CHRISTIAN HEROES: THEN & NOW

JIM ELLIOT

One Great Purpose

CHRISTIAN HEROES: THEN & NOW

JIM ELLIOT

One Great Purpose

JANET & GEOFF BENGE

YWAM Publishing is the publishing ministry of Youth With A Mission (YWAM), an international missionary organization of Christians from many denominations dedicated to presenting Jesus Christ to this generation. To this end, YWAM has focused its efforts in three main areas: (1) training and equipping believers for their part in fulfilling the Great Commission (Matthew 28:19), (2) personal evangelism, and (3) mercy ministry (medical and relief work).

For a free catalog of books and materials, call (425) 771-1153 or (800) 922-2143. Visit us online at www.ywampublishing.com.

Jim Elliot: One Great Purpose

Published by YWAM Publishing
a ministry of Youth With A Mission
P.O. Box 55787, Seattle, WA 98155-0787

ISBN-13: 978-1-57658-146-9 (paperback)
ISBN 978-1-57658-577-1 (e-book)

Ninth printing 2021

Printed in the United States of America

Christian Heroes: Then & Now

Adoniram Judson
Albert Schweitzer
Amy Carmichael
Betty Greene
Brother Andrew
Cameron Townsend
Charles Mulli
Clarence Jones
Corrie ten Boom
Count Zinzendorf
C. S. Lewis
C. T. Studd
David Bussau
David Livingstone
Dietrich Bonhoeffer
D. L. Moody
Elisabeth Elliot
Eric Liddell
Florence Young
Francis Asbury
George Müller
Gladys Aylward
Helen Roseveare
Hudson Taylor
Ida Scudder
Isobel Kuhn
Jacob DeShazer
Jim Elliot
John Flynn
John Newton
John Wesley
John Williams
Jonathan Goforth
Klaus-Dieter John
Lillian Trasher
Loren Cunningham
Lottie Moon
Mary Slessor
Mildred Cable
Nate Saint
Norman Grubb
Paul Brand
Rachel Saint
Richard Wurmbrand
Rowland Bingham
Samuel Zwemer
Sundar Singh
Wilfred Grenfell
William Booth
William Carey

Available in paperback, e-book, and audiobook formats.Unit study curriculum guides are available for select biographies.

www.YWAMpublishing.com

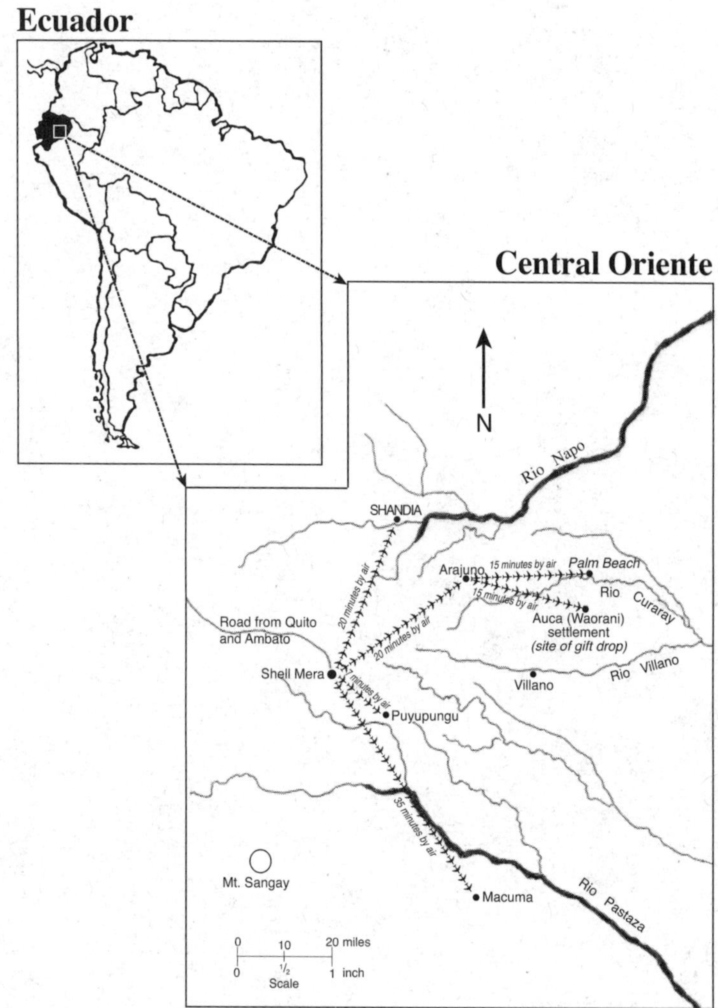

Ecuador
Central Oriente
N
Rio Napo
SHANDIA
Arajuno
15 minutes by air
Palm Beach
15 minutes by air
Rio Curaray
Auca (Waorani) settlement
(site of gift drop)
20 minutes by air
20 minutes by air
Road from Quito and Ambato
Shell Mera
7 minutes by air
Puyupungu
Villano
Rio Villano
35 minutes by air
Mt. Sangay
Macuma
Rio Pastaza
0 10 20 miles
0 1/2 1 inch
Scale

Contents

C er 1

A Day to Remember

For the sixth day, Jim Elliot climbed down thirty-five feet to the ground from the tree house where he had spent a restless night. Wisps of fog hung above the river and snaked among the trees. High above, puffy clouds had massed on the eastern horizon, glowing red and gold as the morning sun crept up behind them to signal the start of another day in the Amazon jungle. A fresh set of paw prints crisscrossed the white sand beach, evidence that a puma had been skulking around the campsite during the night.

Ed McCully and Roger Youderian climbed down from the tree house behind Jim. The three men worked together to get a fire started and a pot of coffee brewing. After a breakfast of coffee, papaya, the three young missionaries opened s and read a psalm together. They talked w it applied to them and their situation the jungle of eastern Ecuador. Then they d their heads and spent time praying together. the time the men had completed their ear-rning routine, the sun had climbed high into the ky and burned off the morning fog. The billowing clouds that had hung over the horizon were now gone. An unusually bright, clear day—at least for this time of year—had settled across the jungle. The three men spent the rest of the morning writing letters to their wives and strolling along the river's edge as they waited for their two companions to arrive.

Around lunchtime, they heard the familiar buzz reverberating above the jungle. Soon the yellow Piper Cruiser was circling over them. The men watched as the plane lined up on the river's edge over the narrow strip of sand they had affectionately nicknamed Palm Beach. The high-pitched whirring of the engine slowed to a medium hum, and then the plane's wheels thumped onto the sand. The Piper pulled to a halt at the far end of the beach, near the tree house. As soon as the engine was cut, Nate Saint, the pilot, and Pete Fleming, his passenger, climbed from the cockpit. Nate was carrying a large picnic hamper, the sight of which cheered Jim, Ed, and Roger. Each day, Ed's wife Marilou sent along with Nate and Pete a delicious treat for the men. This time it was blueberry muffins wrapped in a dishtowel and still hot from the oven. Also tucked into the hamper was a quart of vanilla ice cream that Marilou had made. As the men devoured the muffins and ice cream, Nate and Pete delivered some great news.

While flying from the mission station at Arajuno, Nate and Pete had taken a detour over the Auca Indian settlement, where they had seen only a handful of women and children. About halfway to Palm Beach, they had spotted more Auca Indians—about ten men in a group, walking determinedly toward the missionaries' location. The five men were about to have Auca visitors at Palm Beach. They whooped and hollered with delight as they finished their homemade treat.

Jim Elliot could hardly wait for the visitors to arrive. Today he was going to meet a group of Auca Indians face-to-face; his hope was to share the gospel message with these infamous people. It was the culmination of a dream he'd had for years, a dream that had taken months of careful planning. Sunday, January 8, 1956, was going to be a day to remember, Jim told himself. Since arriving in Ecuador as a missionary in 1952, not a day had gone by that had meant as much to him as today did.

Chapter 2

Full Speed Ahead

It was 2:06 p.m., Saturday, February 2, 1952, the moment that twenty-five-year-old Jim Elliot had been waiting for. Jim watched from the deck of the *Santa Juana* as the stern line that held the freighter snugly against the Outer Harbor Dock in San Pedro, California, was released. Behind him he could hear the groan of a tugboat as the ship edged away from its mooring.

Trying to suppress a huge grin, Jim leaned against the rail and waved to his parents. He could see his mother dabbing her eyes with a handkerchief, and every minute or so his father rubbed a hand over his cheeks. Jim felt a little guilty about being so happy while they were so miserable. His parents were saying good-bye to their youngest son, who was on his way to be a missionary among the Quichua Indians in the jungles of eastern Ecuador, an area shrouded in mystery and superstition. Ever since his first year at Wheaton College in Illinois, where he had graduated with honors, Jim was aware of a strong desire deep inside him to become a missionary. Now, with the throbbing engines of the *Santa Juana* vibrating the deck on which he stood, Jim was finally on his way to living out his dream.

Jim waved again to his parents. His father wore a navy blue suit. His mother had on her best apricot-colored dress and floral hat. Ever since Jim's mother had learned about Jim's desire to be a missionary, she had pointed out that there was plenty of Christian work to do in the United States. Despite his mother's misgivings about his chosen course in life, Jim remembered all the ways his parents had prepared him for what lay ahead.

Fred and Clara Elliot had taught all four of their children the value of independence. From an early age, Jim, his older brothers Bert and Bob, and his younger sister Jane had been given more freedom than most children their age. Jim and his friends loved to go camping and fishing for days, sometimes weeks, at a time. They would collect enough equipment and supplies at the local thrift store and then head into the wilderness around Portland, Oregon, where Jim was born and raised. Jim's parents trusted the boys not to get into trouble and maintained that the trips were a good way for the children to learn responsibility.

Jim's parents also believed that children should work for what they had. There were no free handouts in the Elliot household. There wasn't a lot of money to go around anyway. Jim's father was an evangelist for the Plymouth Brethren Church, and his mother was a chiropractor who worked out of the family home. To make extra money, Jim's older brother Bert had begun recycling long before it became commonplace to do so. Every Saturday, Bert would drive his old truck to the city dump, where he, Jim, and Jim's friend Dick Fisher would rummage through the trash looking for anything that could be resold. The trio would collect bottles and cans and anything else that might have value. They also found items they kept for themselves, such as bricks to build a backyard barbecue with, an old but useful couch, even a bearskin with the head still attached. Jim found a set of strange tools that someone at school told him were used for taxidermy. He was so fascinated by the tools that he took lessons in how to stuff animals. The first thing he stuffed was one of the pesky seagulls that divebombed him at the dump.

The Elliot children's friends had always been welcome in the Elliot home, and with four children, a constant procession of young people marched in and out of the house. Over the years, many missionaries had also visited and stayed with the family. During dinner, Jim would often ask these visitors questions. It was these visits that began to fire his young imagination with the importance and adventure of missionary life.

Jim moved to the aft deck of the *Santa Juana*. The propeller churned the water to a froth as it pushed the ship out into the Pacific Ocean. Jim's parents, still standing on the dock, were now specks on the horizon. Jim waved to them one last time. The next time he would see them he would be the missionary coming home to Portland to visit. He would be the one answering the questions for some curious youngster.

Finally, as San Pedro faded from view, Jim placed his camera carefully back into the leather case that hung around his neck. He glanced at his friend and missionary companion, Pete Fleming. "Well, we're on our way," he said enthusiastically.

Pete adjusted his glasses and grinned. "Yeah, we're on our way, partner!"

Jim liked the word *partner*. Finding a partner to go with him to Ecuador had been hard. He'd thought he'd found the right partner twice before, but both times the arrangement had fallen through. First there had been Bill Cathers, whom Jim first met at Wheaton College. Jim and Bill had renewed their friendship at a Wycliffe Bible Translators Camp they had attended in Oklahoma during the summer of 1950. It was at this camp that Jim had made the final decision to go to Ecuador and had invited Bill Cathers to join him. Bill had agreed, and the two of them had stayed on in Oklahoma for several weeks after the camp was over to see how they would work together as a team. Jim and Bill led Bible studies in a small Plymouth Brethren Church in Oklahoma City. To pay their expenses, they did odd jobs, such as painting houses and fixing fences. Jim and Bill worked well together, and by the end of the six weeks, they were ready to go home, raise the money needed for support on the mission field, and say good-bye to their families and friends.

All along, Jim had been hoping and praying that he and two other men would go to Ecuador together as missionaries. Just as he was about to leave Oklahoma City for Portland, it seemed as though his prayers had been answered. Ed McCully, another friend from Wheaton College, wrote to Jim to tell him that he'd quit law school and was ready to become a missionary.

Jim could hardly believe how well things were falling into place. On his way back to Portland, he stopped off in Milwaukee to visit Ed McCully. Meeting Ed again after a year, Jim was once more struck by his friend's wonderful speaking ability. It was no accident that Ed had won a national oratory award. And while Jim knew that Ed would have made a great lawyer, he was even more excited about what a great missionary his friend would be.

Within weeks of getting back to Portland, however, Jim's plans began to fall apart. First, Bill Cathers wrote saying that he and his girlfriend had decided to get married, and although he still felt he'd be going to Ecuador as a missionary, he wasn't sure a wife would fit into such a primitive setting as living among the Quichua Indians. As a result, he didn't think he should go with Jim.

Jim was even more discouraged when Ed McCully announced plans to marry his girlfriend Marilou. Jim wondered why everything seemed to be going wrong. He was certain God wanted him to go to Ecuador, but now the two partners he had recruited were both getting married. Would he ever find a missionary partner?

Finally, Jim decided that if he could not find someone to go with him, he'd go alone. He began to visit Brethren churches in the United States to raise the financial support he would need to be a missionary. Seattle, Washington, was one of his first stops. There, his old friend Pete Fleming had arranged for him to speak at his local Brethren church, or *assembly,* as it was called. (The Elliot and Fleming families had been friends long before Jim and Pete were born, and from earliest memory, the two boys had played together.)

Jim preached a stirring message at the church in Seattle about missions. In fact, his message was so stirring that it changed the direction of Pete Fleming's life. Until that night, Pete had been planning to go to seminary and then marry his girlfriend Olive. But as he listened to his old friend speak, he became convinced he should go with Jim to Ecuador.

Finally, once he'd given up looking, Jim had the missionary partner he had been praying for. Together, he and Pete set off across the United States. They spoke in churches and Bible studies all the way to the East Coast and back. As they traveled, they became convinced that God wanted to send them out as partners, just as Jesus had sent the disciples out two by two. And now, here they were together aboard ship en route to Ecuador.

As the *Santa Juana* turned south and steamed full speed ahead parallel to the coastline, Jim and Pete made their way down to the cabin they were sharing. Jim arranged some items on the shelf beside his bunk—a photo of his family taken at his brother Bob's wedding, another of his friend Betty, his Bible, and the small, black, leather-bound notebook he'd carried with him everywhere since college. He hardly had to open the notebook; he had read it, preached from it, and quoted from it so many times that he knew its contents by heart. He had begun the notebook when he was a freshman at Wheaton College. In its pages, he had recorded interesting and challenging facts about the mission field. During his second year at Wheaton, he had been asked to speak at some intercollegiate gatherings of the Student Foreign Mission Fellowship. At first he wondered what to speak about, but as he thought about his notebook, he decided to challenge the students with the facts he'd gathered.

Now, as the ship's engine throbbed beneath him and as the smell of salt-laden air drifted in through the porthole, Jim pondered some of the facts recorded in his notebook. There were seventeen hundred languages into which no portion of the Bible had been translated. Ninety percent of Christians who said they wanted to become missionaries never got to the mission field. Sixty-four percent of the people in the world had never heard the name of Jesus Christ. Every hour, 5,000 people died worldwide, making a total of 120,000 deaths a day. There was one Christian worker for every five hundred people in the United States, while the rest of the world averaged one Christian worker for every fifty thousand people. For every man who applied to be a missionary there were eighteen women.

Jim thought about how those facts had motivated him many times. Like a compass, they'd steered him toward his goal. Whenever he had had a spare moment, he had pulled the black notebook from his pocket and considered the facts written in it. He promised himself he would not be one of the 90 percent who didn't make it to the mission field. He wouldn't let anything distract him or stop him. He also thought about the 120,000 people who died every day. If 64 percent of them had never heard of Jesus Christ, that meant that at least 76,800 people died every day without knowing the way to heaven.

When he preached about these facts, Jim always emphasized the need for Christian workers to leave the United States. He told people that since there was one Christian worker for every five hundred people in the United States, and only one for every fifty thousand people in the rest of the world, the United States had one hundred times more Christian workers! Not only that, the United States also had Christian radio shows, books, and records.

Jim pointed out how unfair it was for one country to have so many Christian resources when so many other countries had so few.

Jim had always tried his hardest to convince his fellow students, and others, of the need for missionaries to serve overseas. In the process, he had thoroughly convinced himself that he also had to go. Now, as he drifted off to sleep, rocked gently by the Pacific Ocean, Jim knew he was one of the ten percent who followed through on what they said. He was finally on his way to become a missionary.

The next morning, Jim bounded up the steps two at a time to the aft deck. On his way to the officers' dining room for breakfast, he stopped and peered over the side of the ship. He took a deep breath of the fresh sea air. The wind kicked up small whitecaps on the crests of the waves, and Jim watched as the waves crashed into each other and showered salty froth into the air. He couldn't have been happier. He had dreamed of sailing since he had been in grade school and of going to South America since college. Now, he could hardly believe he was on a ship bound for Guayaquil, Ecuador.

"Come on, dreamer. It's breakfast time," said Pete Fleming, his voice breaking the ocean's spell over Jim.

"It's so easy to forget time out here," replied Jim as he turned to follow Pete to the dining room.

Jim and Pete ate at the captain's table along with the ship's officers and the other seven passengers on board. Over a plate of bacon and eggs, Jim and the captain struck up a conversation. When the captain learned how interested both Jim and Pete were in the ship, he gave them his permission to explore anywhere they liked. But since the vessel was a cargo ship, he warned them to watch out for the derrick booms and winches used to load cargo and move it around in the ship's hold. This equipment could crush a man in a second.

After three days at sea, as the ship was approaching the tropics, Jim began to notice changes in the ocean that delighted him. He chuckled as he watched huge sea turtles lumber past, some of them serving as mini-islands for the gulls perched on their backs. Occasionally, the water churned with schools of flying fish that looped in and out of the water. In the distance, Jim even saw the waterspout of a lone, majestic gray whale. With a click of his camera, he captured the image.

During the voyage, Jim spent as much time as possible speaking Spanish. Most of the crew were from South America, and they were only too eager to laugh at Jim as he attempted to communicate with them. Still, they were patient, and Jim learned a lot from them. The only other exposure he'd had to Spanish was during the six weeks he'd spent in Mexico at the end of his second year of college. Ron Harris, a college friend, had invited him to spend the summer in Mexico with his parents, who were missionaries there.

The six weeks Jim had spent in Mexico were eye-opening. Jim fell in love with the Mexican people and came to see that missionaries were not "special" or superhuman. Instead, missionaries were ordinary people with an extraordinary message to share. Because of the language barrier, Jim had also learned how frustrating it was not to be able to talk to people. He had set out to learn some Spanish as quickly as he could. By the sixth week, he'd learned enough to be able to address a small group of children. The topic he chose was Noah's Ark, and he had a great time miming the animals climbing the gangway into the ark. The children loved listening to the foreigner with the funny accent, and they giggled when he mispronounced a word and filled in for him when he didn't know a word. But giving a five-minute talk to a group of little children and knowing the language well enough to conduct a church service or official business were two very different things.

Jim knew he had a long way to go before he mastered Spanish, the official language of Ecuador. He also knew that Christian Missions in Many Lands, the Plymouth Brethren missionary society he would be serving with, required all its missionaries in South America to speak fluent Spanish before they were sent to their chosen mission stations. So although he was on his way to Ecuador, he still had many challenges ahead of him before he would reach his final destination: the mission station at Shandia in the jungles of eastern Ecuador.

Chapter 3

The Letter

The *Santa Juana* hugged the coastline as it steamed southward past Mexico and on to El Salvador, where it had cargo to deliver. While the ship bobbed at anchor off La Libertad, unloading large crates of goods onto tender boats, Jim, Pete, and four of the other passengers went ashore. The six of them hired a taxi to drive them to San Salvador, the capital city. Although the city was every bit as noisy, busy, and dirty as Jim had imagined it would be, Jim loved every minute he spent there.

With the sightseers safely back aboard, the *Santa Juana* weighed anchor and continued on its journey south. Jim was so busy writing to people back home on the postcards he'd bought in San Salvador that he didn't even notice the coastline of Nicaragua slip by.

The following day, as they steamed past Costa Rica, the captain invited Jim and Pete to go shrimping with him, the chief steward, and the second engineer. Jim helped the second engineer haul the canvas cover off the motorboat that sat in a cradle on the aft deck. Once the cover was pulled clear, the boat was swung overboard by one of the derricks and lowered into the water. Soon Jim, Pete, and the second engineer were joined in the boat by the captain and chief steward, who scaled down a rope ladder lowered over the side of the ship.

The captain had evidently had too much alcohol to drink at lunch and almost immediately fell asleep at the back of the boat. He did not wake up until the boat was ready to be hauled back onto the ship. The other four men, though, had a lively time. They threw out nets behind the boat and hauled in one hundred fifty pounds of the biggest, plumpest shrimp Jim had ever seen. But it wasn't just the shrimp that delighted Jim. The contents of the net were a marine biology exhibit spread out for him to examine. Wiggling in the net were several hammerhead sharks, squid, sharp-toothed corbina, and blowfish, a stingray, a sea cat, and many other weirdly-shaped fish that even the steward could not identify. All in all, the outing was a great success, especially since Jim and Pete had had the opportunity to discuss at length with the second engineer their reason for going to Ecuador.

The final days of the voyage rushed by. The ship skirted the coast of Panama, then Colombia, and finally was steaming down the coast of Ecuador.

The day before they were due to dock, Jim reread the letter he'd received from Dr. Tidmarsh several days before setting sail from San Pedro. Dr. Tidmarsh had expressed his delight that someone was coming to take over the mission base he had established at Shandia. There was still lots of missionary work to be done there. Dr. Tidmarsh also said he would be at the dock in Guayaquil when Jim and Pete arrived and would have airline tickets for them all to fly to Quito.

As Jim read the letter, he couldn't help but think of why he had decided to become a missionary in Shandia, a tiny dot on the map surrounded by dense jungle. Some people called the string of events that had led him to choose Shandia mere coincidence, but Jim believed differently. To him it was the hand of God guiding him toward his destiny.

The first time Jim had even heard of the Quichua Indians and Shandia had been in a letter from his older brother Bert, who had been a missionary in Peru. Tucked inside Bert's letter to Jim was a letter addressed to Bert and signed by a Dr. Wilfred Tidmarsh. As Jim read that letter, he became very excited. Dr. Tidmarsh had been working for many years among the Quichua Indians in eastern Ecuador. He had set up a mission station in the jungle at a place called Shandia and had established a school for boys and a medical clinic. As a result, several Quichuas had become Christians. Dr. Tidmarsh's wife had become ill, however, and was in need of constant medical attention. As a result, the family was going to have to relocate to the city, where Mrs. Tidmarsh could get the medical help she needed. Dr. Tidmarsh was greatly saddened at having to leave the mission station he'd spent so many years establishing. So he had written to Bert in the hopes that Bert might know someone willing to take over the work in Shandia.

By the time Jim had finished reading the letter, his heart was racing. Jim immediately began to respond to the doctor's request. This was just what he'd been waiting for! Fifteen minutes later, the letter offering his services to Dr. Tidmarsh was sealed in an envelope and ready for a stamp. Just then, a thought struck Jim. Instead of asking God whether this was the next move for him, he had presumed it was. He looked at the envelope and shook his head. He knew he could not send that particular letter. But he could write another one, a more general one, asking Dr. Tidmarsh for information about Shandia and the Quichua Indians.

The next time Shandia grabbed Jim's attention was in the summer of 1950 while he was at Camp Wycliffe in Oklahoma City. Camp Wycliffe was an amazing experience for anyone interested in becoming a missionary. Several hundred people attended, staying in university dormitories while the students were in summer recess. Some who attended the camp were older missionaries planning to go into new or unreached areas of the mission field, but most were like Jim, with little or no missionary experience.

Jim loved everything about the camp. Mealtime was filled with interesting conversations about real missionary experiences, and Jim sat in classes with Christian workers from all over the world. Most of all, Jim loved what he was learning in the classroom. Classes were divided into three topics. The first was phonetics, where Jim learned to listen to the different sounds of a language and write them down. Sometimes this was difficult because some languages had gulping, humming, and clicking sounds that were not easy to put in writing using the English alphabet. However, phonetics was an important skill to master, because a missionary who wanted to write in another language would first have to listen carefully and write down the various sounds of the language. Next was morphology class. Here, Jim learned how to find out what words were related to each other in a foreign language. While the English language used prefixes and suffixes to slightly change the meaning of a word, other languages did not, so it was important to know how to discover what words were linked to each other. Finally, there was syntax class, where Jim learned how to discover the way a sentence was put together in a foreign language. All of these classes required a lot of hard study, but Jim enjoyed the challenge.

Once the students had been taught the basics of learning and writing in a foreign language, it was time for them to try out in a real situation what they had learned. To help them do this, the camp organizers had brought in what they called *informants*—missionaries who had lived in remote areas of the world and had mastered little-known languages. Each student was given an informant to work with for a month. It then became the student's task to listen to the language the informant spoke and, using the principles learned in the first half of the school, figure out how the language was put together.

Students waited eagerly to see who their informant would be, and no one was more eager than Jim Elliot. Finally, Jim was introduced to a retired missionary who had been working in Ecuador among the Quichua Indians. Jim could hardly believe it! He began to think it was more than a coincidence that Bert had sent him Dr. Tidmarsh's letter and that he was about to spend a month with a man who had worked with the exact same Indian tribe.

The next few weeks were fascinating for Jim. From his informant, Jim learned that the Quichua Indians numbered a little over 800,000 people but had only five missionaries working among them. Even after all the times he'd preached on the need for foreign missionaries, it was still mind-boggling for Jim to think that there were only five missionaries serving nearly one million people. Something inside Jim stirred. This time he felt more certain that God wanted him to go to the Quichua Indians.

In one of their conversations, Jim's informant mentioned a tribe that Jim had never heard of—the Auca Indians. Jim paid rapt attention as he learned that the Aucas were one of the most difficult tribes in the entire world to reach. The Aucas were a people shrouded in mystery, still living in the Stone Age just miles from one of the most sophisticated oil exploration operations on earth. And they didn't like outsiders, killing most of them on sight. As a result, little was known about the tribe.

Jim could feel the hair on the back of his neck rise as his informant told him all he knew about the Aucas. Jim prayed that one day he might get to meet them himself and play a role in introducing the gospel message to their tribe.

As Camp Wycliffe came to an end, Jim needed to plan for the future. He set aside ten days to pray and ask God for guidance. During this time, little things began to attract his attention. A missionary friend in Africa wrote to say she was praying especially for him because she felt he had an important decision to make. Someone put twenty dollars and an anonymous note in his mailbox. The note read: "God bless you. This is for Ecuador." And his mother forwarded a letter from Dr. Tidmarsh that gave more information about Shandia and the missionary work there.

At the end of the ten days, Jim felt God was indeed calling him to Ecuador—and soon. He wrote to the elders of the Brethren church in Portland, asking if they would sponsor him as a missionary. He also wrote to Dr. Tidmarsh to tell him he was interested in taking over the missionary work at Shandia. Dr. Tidmarsh, who had already moved to

Quito, Ecuador's capital city, was thrilled to hear that someone would be replacing him among the Quichua Indians.

There was one final matter Jim was sure would confirm whether or not God wanted him in Ecuador. It was the matter of the draft board.

Jim's childhood had been lived safely in the midst of a loving family in a tight community. It had been ideal in many ways, except for a single cloud: World War II. The United States had entered the war in 1942, when Jim was fourteen years old, and continued until August 1945, when he was seventeen. During this time, many young men had been drafted into the armed services. But by the time Jim attended Camp Wycliffe in 1950, the war had been over for five years. However, a standoff had developed in Europe between the Soviet Union and the United States and its Allies. The standoff became known as the Cold War. As a result, every young man in the United States over the age of eighteen had to enroll with the draft board and be ready to fight if the need arose. Before he could travel overseas long-term, Jim had to receive permission from the draft board. After waiting anxiously for several weeks, Jim received notice from the draft board that he'd been granted permission to leave the United States.

All of these events, some large, some small, led Jim to where he was right at that moment: a few hours away from the end of his voyage and setting foot in his newly adopted land, Ecuador.

On February 21, 1952, the *Santa Juana* dropped anchor off Puna Island in the Gulf of Guayaquil. Jim and Pete watched as a small yacht, the *Santa Rosita,* tied up alongside the freighter. The captain had already explained to them that no dock in Guayaquil was large enough for the *Santa Juana.* The passengers disembarking there would have to be transferred to a smaller vessel, the *Santa Rosita,* to go ashore while their baggage and other cargo would be transferred to barges and towed in by tugboat. The captain told Jim it would take about four hours for the *Santa Rosita* to make the thirty mile trip up the river to Guayaquil.

Jim and Pete thanked the captain for his hospitality before climbing down the rope ladder slung over the side of the freighter and onto the deck of the *Santa Rosita.* Feeling a surge of excitement, Jim was eager to get ashore and meet Dr. Tidmarsh, who would be waiting for them at the dock.

Jim and Pete stood on the foredeck of the *Santa Rosita* as she plowed her way up the Guayas River. An assortment of boats paraded by—dugout canoes loaded with enormous stalks of bananas or mounds of coconuts, small ferryboats filled with passengers, barges stacked with crates of cargo, and fishing boats with their nets hanging to dry in the hot afternoon sun. Finally, a little more than four hours after leaving the *Santa Juana,* the young missionaries reached the bustling port city of Guayaquil, just south of where the Daule River flowed into the Guayas.

Twenty minutes later, the *Santa Rosita* was tied up firmly alongside the dock, and the passengers began to disembark. Jim stood on deck and scanned the milling crowd for Dr. Tidmarsh, but he could see no white face. Not to worry, by the time he and Pete clambered up onto the dock, Dr. Tidmarsh would emerge from the rear of the crowd. When he did not, Jim and Pete wondered what they should do next.

Chapter 4

Spanish Lessons

An hour passed, and still no sign of Dr. Tidmarsh. Jim wondered what could have happened to him. Dr. Tidmarsh's letter had said he would definitely be there to meet them. Finally, late in the afternoon, Jim and Pete decided the doctor wasn't coming and they had better do something themselves. Jim struck up a conversation with a crewman on the *Santa Rosita,* and the crewman offered to help them find a room for the night. Jim went with him while Pete stayed behind in case Dr. Tidmarsh did show up, and to clear their hand luggage through customs.

An hour later Jim was back. Pete was waiting for him on the dock, having cleared customs without needing to open a single bag. Jim told him he had found them a room for the night in a boarding house run by an elderly German couple. He and Pete hired a man with a wheelbarrow to transport their bags and set off to find their room for the night.

After eighteen days at sea, Jim was thrilled to be greeted by the sights, sounds, and smells of Guayaquil. On the sidewalk were mats spread with brightly colored objects: Panama hats, ponchos, silver jewelry, cocoa beans, and balsa wood models. Squatting by each mat was a man or a woman, bright-eyed and dark skinned, each beckoning Jim and Pete to inspect their wares. Jim wanted to stop to see if he could communicate with them in his limited Spanish, but the sun was setting, and he wanted to get to their destination before dark.

By the time Jim and Pete reached the front door of the guest house, the last glimmer of daylight was fast fading. Inside, the young men gladly accepted the German proprietor's invitation to have dinner with him and his wife. It was nine o'clock by the time they sat down to dine together, and it was still unbearably hot. The proprietor told them it would be hot in Guayaquil every night through April, when the rainy season ended. Jim was glad he was heading for Quito, nestled 9,530 feet above sea level. At that altitude there was no hot, humid wet season to sap a person's energy. Of course, if Dr. Tidmarsh didn't show up the following day, the young missionaries would have to figure out how to get up to Quito on their own.

After dinner, Jim and Pete excused themselves and prepared for bed. It had been a long day, and they needed some sleep.

Jim might have wanted sleep, but it wasn't that easy. The plastic cover on the mattress stuck to him through the cotton sheets, and the tiny room he and Pete were sharing hummed with mosquitoes. The pests seemed to have x-ray vision that allowed them to locate holes in the mosquito net draped over Jim's bed; they bombarded him mercilessly. And then there was the noise. Somewhere in the distance a church clock rang every quarter hour, and the noise of people yelling, mules clopping along on the street, and doors closing seemed to amplify into the room and reverberate off the walls. And when there was no noise from outside, there was the annoying click of the ceiling fan with every rotation.

Finally, after a night of tossing and turning and scratching bug bites, Jim was awakened by the first rays of the morning sun seeping in through the open window. He stumbled out of bed and woke Pete. The two of them ate a quick breakfast with their German hosts and set off for the shipping office to claim the rest of their baggage and cargo that had been brought ashore from the *Santa Juana* by barge and that should now be unloaded. They were also eager to see whether Dr. Tidmarsh had left a message for them. Better than that, Dr. Tidmarsh was waiting for them. The three men shook hands, and the doctor apologized for not meeting Jim and Pete the day before. He explained that the shipping office had given him the wrong arrival date.

Jim and Pete waited patiently for their two tons of baggage and cargo to be cleared through customs. Their bags, boxes, and barrels contained everything the two men thought they might need to start their new lives in Ecuador. Amazingly, no import duties were assessed, and Jim and Pete claimed their belongings. Dr. Tidmarsh arranged for their baggage to be trucked to Quito, and then he pulled three airplane tickets from his coat pocket for the afternoon flight.

As Jim peered out the window of the DC-3 airplane, he was more than relieved that they were flying to Quito and not going by truck. From the air the roads did not look inviting. After leaving Guayaquil, the plane flew over the coastal plain of Ecuador which was divided into huge plantings of green crops with farm buildings and houses dotted among them. With a turbulent bump, the DC-3 then entered a bank of clouds, and when it emerged, the rolling coastal plain had been replaced with the jagged, snowcapped peaks of the Andes Mountains. Jim watched as a narrow valley came into view. He had studied it on the map a thousand times, but it was breathtaking to actually see it spread out beneath him. Tucked in the valley, Quito slowly came into view. The plane circled the city once before coming in to land.

A rush of cool air blasted Jim as he climbed down the steps from the plane and walked across the tarmac. It felt wonderful and refreshing after the steamy air of Guayaquil. Mrs. Tidmarsh was there to welcome Jim and Pete.

From the start, Jim liked Quito. In many ways, it seemed more dignified than Guayaquil. As the men bumped along the city streets in a taxi, Dr. Tidmarsh explained the differences between the two cities. The old Spanish buildings of Guayaquil had all been made of wood and had burned down at various times. By contrast, the buildings of Quito were constructed from huge slabs of stone. The city had been founded in 1534 by a Spanish explorer and was soon the country's main center for trade and culture. Many of the churches and public buildings were nearly four hundred years old.

Jim tried to take everything in. From the taxi, he caught glimpses of quaint, cobblestone courtyards, vivid bougainvilleas trailing over ancient mud walls, and intricately decorated buildings. He could hardly wait to go exploring.

Soon the taxi pulled to a halt outside the gates of the Gospel Missionary Union compound. Dr. Tidmarsh served with the Gospel Missionary Union, and Jim and Pete would stay at the compound until they had mastered Spanish.

Eager to be on their way to Shandia sooner rather than later, the next day Jim and Pete plunged themselves into Spanish lessons. They had a private tutor who was very strict with them and corrected every little mistake they made. Jim didn't mind. He wanted to learn the language as well as he possibly could.

About a month after arriving in Quito, Jim and Pete had the opportunity to visit Dee Short and his family, who were missionaries working among the Colorado Indians at Santo Domingo de los Colorados, seven hours west of Quito. As they bumped along over rutted dirt roads in the back of a pickup, Jim at last felt like a real missionary. In Santo Domingo de los Colorados he followed Dee Short around as Dee gave Bible studies and spoke in churches. Jim even handed out some tracts and, with Dee Short translating, spoke to a group of local schoolboys.

Jim returned to Quito more determined than ever to master Spanish and be on his way to minister to the Quichua Indians in Shandia.

When Jim arrived back at the mission compound in Quito, a letter was waiting for him. Jim immediately recognized the handwriting on the envelope. The letter was from Betty Howard. Excitedly Jim ripped the envelope open. By the time he had finished reading the letter, he thought he would burst. Betty was coming to Quito!

Immediately, Jim set about making preparations for her visit. At the same time, he thought about how he would explain his relationship with Betty to the other missionaries at the compound. In many ways he didn't count Betty as his girlfriend, and they had never officially dated. Jim did not believe in dating. Of course, this had led to some interesting misunderstandings over the years.

Jim thought back to his senior year in high school. He'd been sitting in the cafeteria about to eat lunch with his friend Wayne. Jim had just bowed his head to give thanks for the food when the student president walked up and asked them both to buy tickets to the graduation dance. Wayne had made some excuse about being busy that night, but Jim didn't beat around the bush. "No," he had said flatly. "I'm a Christian, and the Bible says Christians are in the world but not of it. So I won't be going to the dance."

The student president just shook his head and walked away. So many girls had hoped that Jim would invite them to the dance. With his handsome looks, wavy black hair, gray-blue eyes, barrel chest, and rippling muscles, he was considered to be quite a catch—except that Jim had no intention of being caught. Period. In fact, throughout his high school career he never once invited a girl to go anywhere with him—not because he was shy but because he could see no point to it. There were simply more important things to do.

Now Betty was coming to Quito. And while he didn't consider her his girlfriend, Jim nonetheless was caught off guard by how deep his interest in her had grown over the years. The two of them had met in Greek class during Jim's third year at Wheaton College. It had taken Jim a while to realize that Betty was actually the older sister of his college friend Dave Howard. Betty was tall and slim and had a quick mind. She and Jim often studied Greek together or sat for hours in the lower dining hall talking about their faith. Jim marveled as he listened to Betty. For once he had met someone with views as strong as his! Jim and Betty were quite a pair when they didn't agree on something.

In a letter home to his parents, Jim had described Betty as a tall, lean girl who "interested him." But he'd had no intention of taking her on a date. He was single-mindedly focused on becoming a missionary, and he did not have room for distractions. Yet, when Betty graduated a year ahead of him, Jim was surprised at how lonely he felt. Even through his busy senior year, Betty was never far from his thoughts or prayers.

After leaving Wheaton College, Betty attended the same Wycliffe Bible Translator's School as Jim's brother Bert. From there she had traveled to Alberta, Canada, where she worked in a remote area of the province. She and Jim wrote to each other when they had time, but neither of them knew whether their paths would ever cross again. Jim did see Betty once when she visited his family on her way home from Canada.

Now, after much prayer, Betty felt that God was calling her to work in Ecuador. Jim's and Betty's paths were about to cross again, and Jim couldn't have been more pleased. He began planning all the sights he would show her once she arrived. She would love visiting the bustling marketplace and climbing the slopes of Mt. Pichincha. Jim even planned to take her to a bullfight.

Chapter 5

Together Again

April 13, 1952: Jim Elliot waited nervously behind the wire mesh barrier, his eyes focused on the door of the DC-3. The door swung open, and a set of steel steps was wheeled up to it. An elderly man with a cane was the first to appear at the doorway. He wobbled his way down the stairs. Jim leaned forward, easily able to see over the people in front of him. Nine other people climbed out of the airplane, and then Jim's heart skipped a beat. There she was, looking just as he'd remembered her—tall and slim, her dark blonde hair pulled neatly back in a ponytail. Betty Howard descended the stairs and began walking across the tarmac toward the terminal. Jim could scarcely wait for her to reach him outside the terminal building.

The next few weeks zipped by. Although Jim and Betty had continued to write to each other since being students together at Wheaton College, there was something about being able to speak face-to-face. Betty wanted to know how Jim's older brother Bert and his wife were doing. (Bert and his wife were missionaries several hundred miles southeast of Quito in Peru.) Jim was anxious to hear how Betty's younger brother Dave and his wife were doing at their mission station in Costa Rica. Mostly, though, they wanted to hear how the other was doing.

Although they were not officially a "couple," they spent as much time together as they could. Betty fell in love with Quito and its majestic mountain setting, and she and Jim spent many happy hours exploring the place together. They took a bus ride to La Mitad del Mundo, sixteen miles north of Quito, where the equator passes through the middle of town. They rambled through the Mercado de Santa Clara market with its brightly painted balsa-wood birds, cedar statues, bundles of dried herbs, and enormous bunches of freshly cut flowers.

Of course, Jim and Betty kept busy studying Spanish. Most of the places they went, their Spanish tutor went with them, and they would all talk to each other in Spanish the entire time.

They had other studies to occupy their time as well. Though Dr. Tidmarsh was not a medical doctor but was a doctor of philosophy, he had been called on countless times over the years by the

Quichua Indians to act as a medical doctor. Since he had learned as much as he could about jungle medicine, he conducted a course on basic medical procedures for several of the new missionary recruits, including Jim and Pete.

Jim loved the course. Because his mother was a chiropractor, he had been around the medical field most of his life and found it easy learning about everything from leprosy to jungle nutrition and childbirth. By the time he'd finished the course, he could hardly wait to put all his newfound knowledge into practice. He longed to be about the business of being a "real" missionary.

As his months in Quito rolled by, Jim felt that everything was moving much too slowly, especially learning Spanish. A real problem for him was that apart from formal Spanish lessons, he lived in an English-speaking world. Everyone at the Gospel Missionary Union compound spoke and wrote in English; even the newspapers were all English editions. At the rate he was going, Jim figured it would take him a year or more before he would learn enough Spanish to be ready to move to Shandia. That was much too long for his timetable. He needed a way to seclude himself so he would be forced to think and speak in Spanish twenty-four hours a day.

By May Jim had come up with a solution. He had been introduced to a Dr. Cevallos and his wife and seven children. To make ends meet, the family lived in two rooms of their house and rented out the third. Dr. Cevallos offered the room to Jim and Pete to live in. The men gladly accepted the offer. Jim soon found out that living with a Spanish-speaking family sped up his language skills, especially when he practiced with the children, who quickly lost their shyness and happily corrected his mistakes. Jim and Pete also agreed not to talk to each other in English, and soon Jim was even dreaming in Spanish!

The next month, Dr. Tidmarsh offered Jim and Pete the opportunity to get out of Quito for a few days. The mission had undertaken a comprehensive aerial survey of the central Oriente region, and Dr. Tidmarsh asked Jim and Pete if they would like to go to Shell Mera to help with it.

The two of them were thrilled to take part in the aerial survey. The Oriente was the jungle region of Ecuador east of the Andes Mountains. It formed the western reaches of the Amazon Basin. For two thousand miles the jungle ran eastward from Ecuador all the way to the Atlantic Ocean in Brazil. But more important to Jim and Pete, the central Oriente region was where Shandia was located. At last, they would get a chance to see their future home.

The trip to Shell Mera was every bit as torturous as Dr. Tidmarsh had described. The bus bumped and twisted its way south past Mt. Cotopaxi and toward Ambato. Every half hour or so it ground to a halt in a cloud of dust accompanied by excited shouts. Local people either clambered on or off the bus, and the loudness of the shouting depended on how much luggage they had stowed on its roof. Before getting aboard, each passenger heaved onto the bus roof bags, crates, and sacks containing everything from vegetables to bantam hens. It was a lot more difficult, though, to get those things down than it was to toss them up. Sometimes an item of luggage would get stuck at the bottom of the pile, and everything had to be unloaded to retrieve it. It seemed to take forever. Then the mass of passengers would crane to see out the window, making sure all of their belongings were reloaded and not left behind.

Dr. Tidmarsh had warned Jim and Pete not to get off the bus during these stops. There was no scheduled time for the bus to leave a town or village, and if they happened to be too far from the bus when the driver decided it was time to go, they would be left behind without a second thought.

At every stop vendors took advantage of the captive, hungry passengers on board. Of course, Jim and Pete were stand-out targets. The vendors seemed to think the rich gringos would automatically want to buy some of their tasty goodies, everything from homemade lemonade poured into old beer bottles to whole roasted guinea pigs, complete with hair, paws, and teeth.

Finally, at lunchtime, the bus arrived in Ambato, the so-called Gateway to the Oriente. Jim remembered reading about a destructive earthquake that had hit the area three years before, and the damage from it was still visible. Many of the stone buildings lay in ruins or had collapsed roofs. But life seemed to go on despite the damage. Golden brown cocoa beans were spread to dry among the rubble, and small boys ran nimbly over the rocky piles.

From Ambato, the route veered to the east and dropped steeply through the town of Baños, where Jim and Pete bought bananas and mandarins. As the bus moved on into the eastern jungle, the scenery was suddenly completely different. Lush green vegetation laced through with masses of orchids grew right up to the edge of the rutted road.

As the bus bumped along, the snowcapped peak of the volcano Mt. Sangay came into view. Jim studied the map to get their bearings. They were now in the central Oriente and close to their destination, Shell Mera.

Finally, the bus navigated one more dog-legged bend, rolled along for a half mile, and screeched to a halt outside a general store with a sign that read SHELL MERA. They had arrived. Jim felt like pinching himself, first to see whether it was true that he was in the upper reaches of the Amazon jungle and then to see whether he could find some circulation in his numb legs, which had been cramped into the tiny, hard bus seat for thirteen hours!

Jim and Pete were the only ones who got off the bus. Waiting for them was a man who strolled over and shook their hands. He introduced himself as Bob Wittig, the Missionary Aviation Fellowship (MAF) pilot who would be helping them with the survey. Bob led them a short distance back up the road to the MAF station. As they walked, Jim counted about thirty buildings in Shell Mera. From talking with Dr. Tidmarsh, he knew the town had been hacked out of the jungle by the Shell Oil Company, hence its name. The town had served as Shell Oil's base for oil exploration in the Oriente. Three years ago, the company pulled out of the region. It sold most of the buildings at a bargain price to the Gospel Missionary Union, which established the Berean Bible Institute in the buildings to train local Indian Christians.

The road to the MAF station ran parallel to a long, neatly cleared airstrip. At the end of the airstrip, on the other side of the road, stood a tin-roofed house.

"Here we are. This place is a pilot's dream," said Bob Wittig, waving his hand toward the hangar next to the house. Inside the hangar was a four-seat, yellow Piper Pacer aircraft. A trail led from the hangar, across the road, and out to the end of the runway. "Nate knew what he was doing when he set this up," he added admiringly.

The man Bob Wittig was referring to was Nate Saint. Nate had built the house and hangar in 1948 when he arrived in the Oriente to establish a base for Missionary Aviation Fellowship. Nate was a jungle pilot and airplane mechanic, and his wife Marj was an excellent radio operator and hostess. Together they ran the MAF base that serviced a number of mission stations dotted across the surrounding jungle of the Oriente.

Jim had heard great things about Nate and Marj Saint from missionaries in Quito, though he wasn't going to be able to meet them on this trip. They were back in the United States on furlough, and Bob and Keitha Wittig were filling in for them.

Keitha Wittig welcomed Jim and Pete into the MAF house, which was named Shell Merita, meaning "Little Shell Mera." Soon they were all seated on folding chairs and sipping juice. The cool juice was refreshing to Jim after the long bus ride from Quito. As Jim continued to enjoy it, Bob Wittig explained the plan for the survey. He would fly Jim and Pete over large tracts of jungle while they scanned the area for settlements and marked them on a map. Then they would have a better idea of how many Indians lived in the area and where.

It sounded great to Jim and Pete, and the week of surveying sped by. When they were finished, many small and previously unknown settlements were marked on the map. What the men didn't have on their map, though, were any dots showing Auca Indian settlements. The Aucas were the people Jim's informant had told him about two years before at the Wycliffe Summer Institute in Oklahoma City. Only sketchy details were known about this obscure tribe.

Bob Wittig told Jim that two months before, the Aucas had killed a family of five Quichua Indians who had accidentally strayed into Auca territory. The Aucas had a reputation for showing no mercy. Killing seemed to be a way of life for them.

According to Bob, from a very young age the Aucas learned the ways of hatred. Small children were sung lullabies with lyrics based on the names of the people whom that family hated and wanted to kill. No one in a family group was ever allowed to forget whom they had a grudge against. Since every act of murder had to be avenged by another act of murder, a cycle of killing continued unbroken. It was even rumored that in some Auca settlements there was scarcely a person over twenty years of age; all the adults had been murdered.

This just made Jim more anxious than ever to find a way to break that hatred and show the Aucas that there was a better way to live. Still, Jim would have to be patient. He had more Spanish lessons ahead of him before he would be able to return to live in the jungle permanently. And of course, he had been called to work with the Quichua Indians. However, he told himself that while he was doing that, he would keep an eye out for opportunities to reach the Aucas.

Before Jim and Pete headed back to Quito, Bob Wittig flew them over Shandia and pointed out the thatched roof of Dr. Tidmarsh's abandoned house. Since the airstrip was completely overgrown, they were unable to land and take a closer look. Still, at least Jim had an aerial view of his future home fixed in his mind.

Back in Quito, Jim told Betty everything he'd seen and learned in the Oriente. Jim and Pete had seen Shandia! Now they were more eager than ever to master the language and make the move to their new location. With but a single obstacle keeping them in Quito, Jim and Pete threw themselves into their Spanish lessons with renewed determination.

At the end of July, five months after arriving in Quito, Jim and Pete got some great news. According to Dr. Tidmarsh, they had made such good progress learning Spanish that they didn't need a whole year of lessons. It was time for them to start making plans to move to Shandia.

In preparation, Jim and Pete sorted through all the equipment and supplies they had brought with them from the United States. Since they wouldn't be able to take everything with them to Shandia at once, they sorted out those things that would be useful immediately and placed them into two backpacks and two other bags. The rest of their belongings were stored away at the Gospel Missionary Union compound.

While Jim and Pete were getting ready to move to Shandia, Betty was making plans of her own. She had heard of the need for missionaries who could translate the Bible into the Colorado Indian. To help with the translation work, she and her newly assigned partner, Doreen, would live in San Miguel, a remote village about a fifteen-hour drive west of Quito on the other side of the Andes Mountains.

Much to his dismay, Jim learned that it would take a letter about six weeks to get from Betty in San Miguel to him in Shandia. He wished she would be stationed somewhere closer and more accessible, but he knew that like him, Betty had been called to work among the Indians of Ecuador and must go where God was leading her. Still, he had enjoyed having her close by during their stay in Quito. Now it was time to do what God had called him to: minister to the Quichua Indians in Shandia.

Chapter 6

Shandia at Last

At 6:00 a.m. on Friday, August 15, 1952, an overloaded bus lurched out of the marketplace in Quito. As it began its twisted downhill trip to Shell Mera, Jim Elliot perched quietly in one of the narrow, hard seats. Beside him sat a young boy who looked shyly out the window. He was one of eighteen boys from Quito whom Jim and Pete were escorting to Shell Mera, where they would all participate in a week-long boys' camp. After helping with the camp, Jim and Pete would move on to Shandia.

As the bus rumbled along, Jim tried to sort through his feelings. On the one hand, he was excited. He was finally on his way to live in Shandia, and he relished the challenge that lay ahead. After six months of sitting around in Quito learning Spanish, he was finally going to be a missionary.

In spite of being excited about what lay ahead, Jim felt sad. Yes, every mile the bus carried him away from Quito was a mile closer to Shandia, but it was also a mile farther away from Betty. Jim had risen extra early that morning just so he could walk one last time past the house where she was staying. He had wanted to yell up to her window to see if she was awake. In the end, he had just stood there and said a silent good-bye. Now that he was on his way to Shandia on the east side of the Andes Mountains while Betty was going to San Miguel on the west side, he wondered when they would see each other again.

The bus wound its way past Mt. Cotopaxi, shrouded in swirling morning mist, and then headed south through Ambato and Baños until finally, late in the afternoon, it screeched to a halt in Shell Mera.

As Jim and Pete and the eighteen boys scrambled from the bus, Dr. Tidmarsh was waiting for them. He had come down to Shell Mera several days earlier to help set up the boys' camp. As Jim walked around the bus a couple of times to get the circulation in his legs going, the bus driver climbed onto the roof of the bus and unloaded their belongings. Jim checked to make sure all the bags were there, and when he indicated they were, the bus disappeared in a cloud of dust. Jim and Pete and Dr. Tidmarsh led the boys to the Berean Bible Institute, where the camp was to be held.

Jim enjoyed his week at camp. Everyone arose at 6:00 a.m., when they had "café," a light breakfast of sweet-bread rolls and hot chocolate. After café, it was on to group Bible study and singing, followed by a morning snack of bananas and roasted corn kernels. Then it was time for a team game. Soccer was the boys' favorite. After lunch, they took a *siesta,* or nap, compensation for getting up so early. When siesta was over, everyone went swimming in a stream about ten minutes away. After dinner there was another short Bible study, and then it was bedtime.

When Jim wasn't with the boys, he was following Nate Saint around, trying to gain every piece of practical advice he could about living in the jungle. Nate and his wife Marj had lived in Shell Mera since 1948.

Jim was particularly interested in Nate's garden. He took cuttings from some of the most successful plants growing there and stowed them away meticulously in his backpack for the trip to Shandia. By the end of the week, he had collected, among other things, rose, geranium, and hibiscus cuttings; coffee bean plants; poinsettia seedlings; and a variety of orchid roots. Jim was itching to start his first tropical garden when he finally moved to Shandia.

One week after the group had arrived in Shell Mera, the sun rose golden across the eastern jungle. Jim was brimming with excitement as he loaded his belongings into MAF's Piper Cruiser, which Nate had just flown to Shell Mera from the United

States. The plane was painted the same distinctive yellow as the other MAF plane, a Piper Pacer, in which Jim had flown during the aerial survey. Nate carefully supervised the loading of the plane. He made sure the weight of their heavy backpacks and other belongings was distributed evenly in the back. When they had loaded enough for the first trip, Pete and Dr. Tidmarsh climbed in. They would fly to Pano, northeast of Shell Mera, and then Nate would return for Jim and the rest of their belongings.

Nate cranked the engine of the Piper Cruiser until it burst to life. The engine purred smoothly while Nate checked his instruments. Nate set the flaps and revved the engine slightly, and the plane crawled forward. Nate taxied across the road to Ambato and out to the end of the runway. As Jim watched, Nate gunned the engine, commanding the yellow plane to pick up speed and race down the runway. Moments later, the Piper was clear of the ground and climbing into the still, morning air. It banked to the left and headed away from Shell Mera. Jim watched until the plane had vanished in the brilliant glow of the morning sun.

About one and a half hours later, the buzz of Nate's plane filled the air as Nate circled around Shell Mera and came in for a landing. As soon as the yellow plane taxied to a halt in front of the MAF hangar, Jim began to load up the last of the cargo. Soon he and Nate were aloft, zipping along above the jungle, headed to Pano, the nearest airstrip to Shandia. As Jim watched the mass of green vegetation pass below, he marveled at the ease and convenience of flying. It would take the plane about twenty-five minutes to cover the thirty-five miles to Pano. Nate explained to Jim that the same journey on foot would take several days of difficult hiking through dense jungle. Jim now understood why Dr. Tidmarsh had told him that clearing and repairing the overgrown airstrip at Shandia needed to be their first priority.

As the MAF plane glided effortlessly above the lush jungle, Jim thought about all that lay ahead. Dr. Tidmarsh was going to lead them overland to Shandia from Pano and then spend a month with them while Jim and Pete set things up. It certainly seemed that they were going to be busy right from the start. Dr. Tidmarsh had plans for them to build another house next to the one already there after they cleared and repaired the airstrip. In addition, several other buildings were badly in need of repair. And then there was the boys' school to reopen. On top of all this, Jim would need to learn the Quichua language. Even though some of the Quichuas could understand Spanish, Dr. Tidmarsh had informed Jim and Pete that learning the local dialect as quickly as possible was vital to the success of their ministry.

The sharp banking turn of the Piper Cruiser snapped Jim back to the moment at hand. Nate trimmed the plane and set the flaps and throttle for landing. To Jim, the jungle seemed to be rising ominously close to the plane, but Nate didn't seem at all concerned. Right about the time Jim expected the tops of the trees to start slapping the bottom of the plane, a clearing appeared. About fifty feet past the edge of the clearing, the wheels of the Piper abruptly touched down on the ground. The whole plane vibrated as Nate cut back on the throttle and guided the plane to the end of the airstrip where Pete was waiting with Dr. Tidmarsh and a group of Indians he had hired to help carry their belongings. As soon as Nate cut the engine, Jim jumped out of the plane and began unloading the gear.

After saying good-bye to Nate Saint, the three men hoisted their overstuffed packs onto their backs while the Indians divided up the rest of the belongings. The party then set off for Shandia, a three-hour trek from Pano. Jim fell in step behind Pete, while Dr. Tidmarsh led the way. The Indians followed behind Jim.

In the jungle, huge kapok trees towered above, providing shade not only for the travelers but also for an amazing array of mosses and lichens. Giant air ferns clung to the trunks of the trees, and translucent butterflies fluttered casually down the long, narrow trail.

Occasionally, Dr. Tidmarsh signaled for the group to stop. When they did, Jim would sometimes catch a glimpse of a multicolored snake slithering into the undergrowth. Birds squawked around them, and often when Jim looked up, he would see spider monkeys swinging casually from tree to tree. As he trudged over huge tree roots and around muddy pits, he wished he could swing freely like the monkeys above.

Dr. Tidmarsh kept glancing at his watch. He was pleased with the time they were making, but he kept reminding Jim and Pete to keep up their pace. Finally, as golden late-afternoon sunlight filtered lazily through the green canopy above them, the thin trail widened out into a man-made clearing. At the far end of the clearing overlooking a steep bluff stood a simple split-bamboo hut. "Here we are," announced Dr. Tidmarsh cheerfully. "Home, sweet home."

As he spoke, several figures emerged from the trees at the edge of the clearing. With shouts of recognition they raced up to Dr. Tidmarsh and threw their arms around him. Jim smiled as they chattered away in the Quichua language. He supposed they were telling Dr. Tidmarsh all that had happened since he'd left. They seemed to speak at breakneck speed, interspersing their conversation with loud rounds of laughter. As he listened to Dr. Tidmarsh, Jim hoped he would soon be able to speak Quichua as fluently as the doctor.

After fifteen minutes of joyous conversation, the Quichua Indians escorted the three missionaries to the far end of the clearing where the tall hut stood on piles three feet off the ground. Jim, who had seen the structure only from the air, was surprised at how high its thatched roof was. The roof sat like an oversized hat, twice as high as the walls that supported it.

"This is where I lived with my family," said Dr. Tidmarsh looking at the hut. "It's in better condition than I'd expected. Let's see what it's like inside."

The three of them climbed the wooden steps that led inside. The interior was surprisingly large. The living area was divided from the sleeping area by a ceiling-to-floor curtain. A couple of rugs covered the floors, but they were littered with dead bugs. Jim, who'd expected the house to be in much worse condition, strolled into the sleeping area and laid down his backpack.

The Indians deposited the rest of the gear in the living area while Dr. Tidmarsh lit a Coleman stove. The small stove burst to life with a hiss. "I thought we'd have some canned baked beans for dinner," he said with a smile. "But don't worry, tomorrow I'll show you how to eat like a local!"

Jim grinned. He knew Dr. Tidmarsh would enjoy watching him eat jungle foods for the first time, especially the foods that wiggled!

An hour later, the three of them had eaten dinner and cleaned up. Now it was time for bed. It had been a long, exhausting day. Jim took one last look from the screened window before turning in for the night. The silver reflection of the moon danced on the surface of the Atun Yaku River, which flowed swiftly along at the bottom of the bluff. The whole scene was even more beautiful than Jim had imagined it would be. Jim rolled out his sleeping bag and lay down on top of it. It was much too hot to crawl inside. He lay on his back for a long time listening to the symphony of sounds around his new home. A troop of monkeys squawked in the distance, a bird made raucous calls from a nearby tree, and the low rumble of water from the river filled the night with a soothing monotone.

When Jim awoke the next morning, a broad smile spread across his face. Jim Elliot was about to begin his long-awaited first day of missionary work in the jungle.

Jim studied the hut he had just spent the night in and tried to think how to describe it to Betty in a letter. It was nowhere near as modern as the MAF house in Shell Mera, but it was comfortable none-theless. The walls were made from split bamboo, and the floors from wood planks. The ceiling consisted of thick tar paper nailed to the rafters. As the men ate pineapple and rice porridge for breakfast, Dr. Tidmarsh explained that huge bats lived in the high peak of the roof. The tar paper stopped bat droppings from landing on people or in a plate of food or a glass of beverage. Jim was grateful for the paper as he sipped his coffee.

The next few days were a blur of new experiences and images. Just as he had promised, Dr. Tidmarsh introduced Jim and Pete to jungle food. Jim was able to stomach most things; he even enjoyed some of them. He ate heart of chonta palm—similar to the nutty flavor of a chestnut—papaya, avocado, all shapes and colors of banana-related fruits, hierba luisa (a green tea made from jungle leaves), and a fat chonta worm. He managed to swallow the worm, but just barely. Dr. Tidmarsh, though, smacked his lips with delight after eating half a dozen of them!

Their first undertaking was to start the job of reclaiming the overgrown airstrip. It was a huge task and would take a number of weeks to complete. To help with the task, Dr. Tidmarsh hired about twenty Quichua men with machetes. The workers approached the job enthusiastically, although their enthusiasm didn't stop some of them from wandering off into the jungle for unofficial breaks. Keeping track of the men and keeping them working was a full-time job. But Dr. Tidmarsh knew how to talk with them.

The days quickly fell into a pattern. Not wanting to waste any natural light, the three missionaries would rise at 6:00 a.m., soon after the sun rose. They would sit outside and shave on the steps one at a time. As they did so, a group of Indians would gather around to watch. Someone in the group would mimic their actions, pretending to skim a razor over his chin and cheeks. Howls of laughter would follow from the others.

Some of the Indians would stay and watch the trio eat breakfast, which usually consisted of fresh fruit and a stick of steamed manioc, topped off with a mug of good strong coffee.

At first, Jim found the lack of privacy difficult. Wherever he went and whatever he did, there always seemed to be someone there staring or giggling. But telling the Quichuas that staring or giggling was rude would have achieved nothing; they simply didn't have the same need for privacy as Jim and Pete had. Jim knew he was the one who would have to adjust to the situation.

After breakfast, at 7:15 a.m., it was time to call Marj Saint on the handcranked radio. The men would let her know that everything was fine and give her a list of supplies they needed flown in. Of course, until they got their airstrip cleared, supplies would have to be flown to Pano and collected from there by foot, a trek of six hours roundtrip.

When radio contact ended, the three men would study the Bible and pray for a while. Dr. Tidmarsh would then set out to gather the workforce for the day while Jim and Pete passed the time studying Quichua. Learning the language wasn't easy at first, but the men pressed on because soon they would be on their own, without the benefit of Dr. Tidmarsh's knowledge of the language.

Throughout the rest of the day, the men would alternate between supervising the workers and studying the language. Wherever they went, Jim and Pete would carry a notebook and pen to write down new Quichua words to learn. As they worked on getting the Quichua school back in order, Dr. Tidmarsh had a teacher flown in to teach the students once classes resumed.

Dr. Tidmarsh's month with Jim and Pete passed quickly. The young missionaries bade Dr. Tidmarsh good-bye as he set out for Pano to be flown back to Shell Mera. They were sad to see him go, but they knew he would be back. The doctor planned to return at regular intervals to stay with Jim and Pete and help their ministry along.

On September 30, several days after Dr. Tidmarsh had left, Jim and Pete rose earlier than normal to make a final inspection of the newly cleared runway. They checked to make sure there were no holes unfilled or rocks left on the tiny airstrip. When they were satisfied that everything was in order, they walked back to their hut for breakfast. At 7:15 a.m. they made their regular call to Marj Saint. Excitedly, Jim told Marj that the airstrip at Shandia was finished and ready for use.

By early afternoon, nearly one hundred fifty Quichua Indians had gathered with Jim and Pete beside the airstrip and were anxiously waiting. They heard Nate Saint's Piper Cruiser long before they could see it. The plane flew in low from the southwest. Nate banked into a tight turn and circled the new runway twice, checking it out before attempting to land. When he was satisfied that everything was in order, he lined his plane up for a landing. Jim watched as the wheels thumped down onto the new airstrip and the plane glided to a halt. As soon as Nate cut the engine, the crowd surrounded the plane and helped unload the goods he had on board for the missionaries. After twenty minutes on the ground, Nate took off to service the other mission stations in the Oriente.

Jim went to sleep that night very content and relieved that they now had a direct lifeline to the outside world.

Chapter 7

Losses and Gains

"Get up! Get up! Come with me," pleaded a voice in Quichua through the darkness of a moonless November night.

Jim awoke with a start. Someone was frantically shaking him. Jim sat up in bed. He couldn't make out who the man was, but from the urgency in the voice, he realized it must be an emergency.

Jim leapt out of bed and lit the kerosene lamp. "Hey, Pete, get up. There's some kind of trouble out there," he said shaking Pete awake.

"What is it?" asked Pete drowsily.

"I don't know. I figure we'll take the medical bag and follow this man," Jim told him.

Both men pulled on some clothes, and within five minutes of being awakened, they were following the

Indian man on a lightly trodden path that ran along the riverbank. Jim flipped on a flashlight that gave some light but also caused eerie shadows to dance over the path. An animal screeched in the darkness, and Jim heard the leaves near his feet rustle. He dared not put his hand on a branch to steady himself for fear he might grab a snake.

After ten minutes of rushing along at a speed somewhere between fast walking and jogging, the men stopped in front of a small hut. Although Jim didn't recognize the man who had guided them there, he did recognize the hut as one he'd visited a week or so before. There seemed to be a lot of activity inside. Jim and Pete followed the Quichua man into the hut. Once inside, the Quichua man led them over to a three-month-old baby girl lying in a hammock. The baby lay still; her eyes were open but vacant. Jim set the medical bag down and touched the baby's forehead. "Poor little thing, she's burning up with fever," he muttered.

Pete walked to the other side of the hammock and stared down at the baby while Jim placed a thermometer under her armpit. The mercury shot up to 104 degrees Fahrenheit. There was little else the two of them could tell about the baby's condition.

As Jim slipped the thermometer back into his bag, the Indian man who had led them to the hut pulled on Jim's shirt sleeve and acted out injecting the baby with a syringe.

Jim nodded. He knew that the Indians thought that syringes were white people's cure for every illness. In the past, whole tribes of Amazon Indians had been wiped out through contact with European diseases. Typhoid, even the common flu, had killed hundreds of thousands of people who had no previous exposure to or immunity from such diseases. But the same people who had inadvertently brought such diseases to the Indians had also brought relief in the form of antibiotics and vaccines. And since these medicines were usually administered with a syringe, the Indians had come to trust syringes.

"What do you think?" Jim asked Pete about the baby's condition.

"My guess is she has pneumonia. I think we should give her an antibiotic shot now and maybe another one in a few hours."

Jim nodded. He had arrived at the same conclusion.

"And," Pete continued, "if she isn't any better in the morning, we can radio Marj Saint and have Nate transport her to Shell Mera. Marj will have a better idea than us about what to do next."

Jim nodded and broke the seal on a vial of penicillin. He drew the liquid up into the syringe and rolled the limp little girl over before gently jabbing the needle into her buttocks. Her body tensed, but the baby did not cry. The Indian man then pointed to a corner where some roughly made split-bamboo platforms stood.

"Sleep?" Jim asked in Quichua.

"Yes," said the man.

Jim and Pete lay down on the platforms to sleep until morning. About an hour later, they were awakened by a series of high-pitched whistles and pops. Jim turned his head slowly and opened his eyes without making a sound. Through flickering firelight he could see the local witch doctor bending over the child. Jim heard him spitting and coughing over the little girl, and then the witch doctor began to chant and blow circles of smoke in the baby's face.

Everything within Jim made him want to jump up and chase the witch doctor away. Nothing that "doctor" was doing could possibly help the girl, and the last thing she needed was someone blowing smoke in her face. Jim wished he knew enough of the Quichua language to properly share the gospel message with these people. He prayed silently until he again dozed off on the uncomfortable platform. It was three o'clock when he next awoke. Muffled gasps were coming from the direction of the baby girl's hammock. Jim quickly jumped up and raced over to her. The gasps stopped. He felt her; she was still warm but no longer breathing. Desperately he searched for a pulse, but he couldn't find one. He began mouth-to-mouth resuscitation. *Puff. Puff. Puff.* "Out, one, two, three," he counted over and over to himself.

Several minutes later, Jim gave up. The baby girl's body was becoming cold, and Jim knew it was pointless to keep trying to revive her. There would be no emergency flight to Shell Mera, no hospital, no second chance for her. With a heavy heart he turned to the parents, who had already begun calling other Indians from their huts.

By seven o'clock in the morning the funeral was well under way, but it was not like any other funeral Jim had ever attended. At this funeral, all of the "mourners" were happy and laughing. A group of men at the back of the hut were crowded around a game of checkers being played on a board etched on the dusty floor, with nuts as game pieces. Every few minutes, the men would erupt into howls of laughter. The louder the grieving mother sobbed, the louder the men laughed.

Jim and Pete stepped outside for a few minutes. The rays of the early morning sun slanted through the trees above. "I guess this is what Dr. Tidmarsh meant," said Pete, shaking his head.

"I guess so," replied Jim. "It sure is hard to get used to."

The men pondered the silence for a while. Jim didn't have the energy to go back into the hut and be "happy" again, yet he knew it was customary for Quichua mourners to laugh and joke as a way of taking a family's thoughts off their dead relative. Jim wondered what his folks would say if they saw him acting like he was at a party while a dead baby girl lay gently swinging in a hammock in the corner.

Despite being desperately tired and lacking energy, the two missionaries finally went back inside. Both Jim and Pete understood the importance of sharing different experiences with the Indians, and a funeral like this was definitely a different experience.

Jim and Pete watched as a new game was played. In this game, a bowl of milky white liquid was placed in front of a man who then sat cross-legged and grasped the rim of the bowl in his teeth. With a swift action, the man whipped the bowl back over his head, its liquid contents splashing onto the floor behind him. A second man sat down. The bowl was refilled and its rim placed between the man's teeth. With a flick of the head, this man too sent the bowl reeling backward, but not fast enough. The liquid from the bowl splashed all over him. The other men howled with laughter and then pointed to Jim. Their challenge was obvious—would he try?

Jim had been concentrating hard on the technique of the game, so he nodded and sat down. The room went silent. All eyes settled on the white missionary sitting cross-legged holding a bowl rim between his teeth. Jim concentrated for a moment, and then, with a fast and sudden jerk of his head, he sent the bowl and its liquid contents hurtling backward. The bowl shot across the room and hit the wall, sending the liquid cascading to the ground. The men cheered. "Pacha!" they yelled.

A broad smile settled across Jim's face. Jim knew the word was the local equivalent of *wow*, and he was proud of his new skill. Of course, the men didn't know that years of wrestling had given Jim excellent coordination. They were surprised that an outsider could master their game.

An hour later the two missionaries excused themselves and returned to their hut, where Jim made a tiny coffin from a crate used to transport radio parts to Shandia. As the late afternoon sun sank, Jim and Pete helped bury the baby girl behind the schoolhouse.

It had been a long day, and Jim fell into bed that night exhausted. As he drifted off to sleep, he thought about the letter he'd received a few days before from Ed McCully. According to the letter, Ed had finished a year-long course at the School of Missionary Medicine in Los Angeles, and he, his wife Marilou, and their eight-month-old son Steve were planning to join the team in Shandia. The whole family planned to be in Quito by Christmas and in Shandia as soon as they had learned enough Spanish.

Jim was very excited by the letter. He had thought that Ed would settle down after he got married and not want to do missionary work. Instead, Ed wanted to be a missionary with Jim and Pete at Shandia. After the day's events, Jim felt great relief at the thought of Ed's taking over the medical work. Maybe Ed would have been able to save the baby girl's life.

The more Jim thought about Ed and Marilou McCully joining the team in Shandia, the more he began to see the advantages a married couple would have working together on the mission field. A woman could talk to the Indian women more easily and would be a natural choice to help with childbirth. Jim also thought about how, in Marilou, Ed had his best friend with him for company. He began to feel a little envious. He would love to have Betty working at his side.

In January 1953, Jim was scheduled to visit Quito for a two-week missionary conference, though he had mixed feelings about leaving Shandia. He and Pete had made many good friends among the Quichua Indians, and the ministry work was moving ahead as planned. The airstrip was finished, and the school was up and running for boys grades one through four. Early on, Dr. Tidmarsh had hired a Quichua schoolteacher, relieving Jim and Pete of having to teach using their growing but limited grasp of the Quichua language. An electric generator had also been flown in and hooked up, providing a source of electricity, even though, due to the cost of fuel, it ran only three times a week. All this combined to make Shandia a comfortable place to call home.

Even though Jim was reluctant to leave, especially since Pete would be running everything alone, he knew he had to go. In the previous few weeks, Jim had decided to do something he'd never done before: propose marriage to Betty!

Once he arrived in Quito, Jim quickly realized he had made the right decision to leave Shandia for two weeks. It was energizing to be around other missionaries, and it was fun to be communicating in English again. He also wasted no time sending a telegram to Betty. He was sure the message would leave her guessing. It simply read: "Meet me in Quito. Love, Jim."

While he waited for Betty to arrive, Jim had lots to do. Ed McCully had arrived in Quito the month before, and he and Jim had much news to catch up on. Jim also met Ed's wife Marilou and now nine-month-old Steve. When Jim saw Ed in Quito, he was reminded of the first time they'd met. It had been at Wheaton College, when Jim was president of the Foreign Missions Fellowship. Jim had challenged each member of the fellowship to target five other students for whom to pray. Jim chose five people he thought would make excellent missionaries, including the senior class president, Ed McCully. Ed had everything going for him. He was a brilliant student, a star player on the football team, holder of the college record for the 220-yard dash, and winner of a national oratory competition. Also, Ed was not one bit interested in being a missionary. His sights were set on becoming a lawyer.

Although Jim had prayed faithfully that Ed would rethink his career choice and become a missionary, Ed's career path did not change. Indeed, Jim had been deeply disappointed when Ed left Wheaton and went off to law school at Marquette University. The two of them, though, had kept in touch by letter. Now, miraculously, the person Jim had prayed would become a missionary was in Quito learning Spanish and preparing to work among the Quichua Indians.

Three days after Jim sent the telegram, Betty arrived in Quito. She had ridden a horse from her mission station to Santo Domingo, where she had hitched a ride to Quito on a truck hauling bananas. The bumpy ride had taken her ten hours.

Betty was eager to find out why Jim had mysteriously summoned her. That night, beside the fireplace in the Tidmarsh house, Jim Elliot asked Betty Howard to marry him sometime in the not too distant future. First, he explained to Betty that he had to build a house for the McCullys, and then he reminded her that she would need to learn the Quichua language. Betty accepted his proposal with joy!

Although they spent ten wonderful days together, the time raced by, and the two of them now had to go their separate ways. Jim packed for the flight to Shandia, and Betty prepared for the journey to the western jungle to continue her translation work in the Colorado language and to figure out some way to learn the Quichua language— quickly!

Soon after they parted, Betty wrote to Jim that her time helping to record and translate the Colorado language was almost at an end. She planned to organize her files, charts, and notebooks and hand them over to her partner Doreen, who would continue the painstaking work.

A month later, Betty moved in with the Conns, a missionary family who lived at Dos Rios on the edge of Quichua territory. Everyone in the Conn family spoke fluent Quichua and promised to help her learn the language as quickly as possible. Betty wanted to do whatever she could to hurry along her wedding day.

Betty had been with the Conns only a week when she received a letter from Doreen. All of Betty's language notes and files on the Colorado language were gone. They had been in a suitcase that Doreen had put on top of a bus en route to Quito. When Doreen went to retrieve the suitcase, it was gone, and with it a year's worth of Betty's work. Betty was devastated. Everything had been handwritten, and there was no backup copy. Betty wrote to Jim and told him the terrible news, but she didn't expect him to understand what it felt like to lose a whole year's work.

Indeed, at that moment, Jim might not have understood what it felt like to lose a year's labor, but he soon would.

Chapter 8

The Angry River

June 14, 1953: Jim Elliot sat writing by the light of a kerosene lamp. "This may become known as the season of the big flood," he wrote in his journal. Several of the older Quichua men helping with the construction of the new house for the McCullys had told him it was the worst flooding they had seen in thirty years. The rain had poured down without interruption for five days. Being from Oregon, Jim was used to rain, but nothing could have prepared him for the torrential sheets of water that now fell from the sky. It was impossible to get away from the noise of pelting rain and the thunderous roar of the swirling, flooded Atun Yaku River at the bottom of the bluff. It was also impossible to go more than a few steps outside without getting soaked to the skin. And it was too wet to continue work on the McCullys' new house, which was painfully near completion.

The construction had seemed to drag on, but now a fine-looking new home sat adjacent to Jim and Pete's hut on top of the bluff. It had been built of the best materials. It was perched on concrete piles and was clad with sturdy wood planks and had an iron roof. Between the new house and the schoolhouse, which sat about one hundred yards back from the edge of the bluff, the men had also built a new medical clinic. For Nate Saint to fly in the materials for these new buildings, they'd had to clear more jungle and extend the length of the airstrip.

The rain was pounding when Jim turned off the kerosene lamp and headed for bed. It was still pounding when he awoke the next morning and peered out the screened window toward the river. He could barely see a thing through the deluge, but he could hear the angry roar below. The last time Jim had checked, the river was flooding high above its normal level, and its surging waters were carrying away huge trees and other vegetation that had been ripped out by their roots from along the riverbank.

Jim sighed deeply. There would be no work on the McCullys' new home today. Just another day of inside work. Still, before he settled down, Jim needed to check on some things outside. He slipped on a raincoat and opened the door. A wall of water was cascading off the roof, and Jim was drenched before he even reached the bottom of the steps. The first thing Jim wanted to check was the small generator shed, which housed the generator for the school and the new clinic. As he battled the rain, Jim recalled the excursion he and Pete had made two days before. They'd followed the trail down the river until, without warning, the riverbank fell sharply away directly in front of them. A chunk of rock and sand larger than a football field disappeared into the swollen river.

The power of the swirling river had amazed Jim. By the time he'd returned to Shandia he was a little worried. Since the generator shed sat on the edge of the bluff above the river, he had tied one end of a thick rope to the generator and the other end to the sturdy orange tree that grew in front of their hut. Jim didn't think the bluff would give way, but he wasn't going to take any chances.

Now, as the rain continued to beat down relentlessly, Jim wanted to make sure all was still well. Through the sheets of rain he couldn't seem to make out the shape of the generator shed. When he touched the rope he understood why. It was stretched taut. Jim picked up his pace, sliding his hand along the rope as he went. Suddenly, the rope disappeared over the edge of the bluff, which was now about ten yards closer to the house than it had been. The land on which the generator shed had stood was gone, and the generator was dangling in midair, swinging above the angry waters of the Atun Yaku River.

Quickly, Jim ran back to the house to get Pete. They rounded up several Quichua men, and the group heaved on the rope until the generator was safely back on the bluff. Someone slid two planks of wood under the generator to act as skids, and they all dragged the generator back beside the schoolhouse, where Jim hoped it would be out of harm's way. But what about the other buildings? When they had laid the foundation for the McCullys' new house, Jim had assumed it was far enough from the edge of the bluff. Now he wasn't so sure.

Cautiously, Jim made his way over to the nearly completed house. The good news was it was still standing. But the bluff had crept within fifteen yards of the front door, half the distance it had originally been. There was little Jim could do but hope and pray that no more of the bluff eroded. Jim began retreating to his house to get out of the rain, until he noticed with alarm that the edge of the bluff had advanced just as close to his own hut.

Inside, Jim and Pete wondered out loud what might happen if the rain didn't stop in the next couple of days. Many hours of labor had gone into building the McCullys' new house. The wooden planks on the side of the building had been painstakingly overlapped and nailed in place, and the concrete had been hand mixed and poured into forms to make the piles. The roofing iron had been flown in by Nate Saint a few sheets at a time, slung under the belly of his yellow Piper Cruiser. And now, just a few days short of completion, the whole structure was in danger of being destroyed.

The more they discussed it, the more Jim knew what had to be done. He just wished he didn't have to undertake such a mammoth task in the midst of the torrential rain. He and Pete and a group Quichua workers were going to have to carefully tear down the McCullys' new house and stack the building materials away from the edge of the bluff.

When Jim told Pete what had to be done, Pete was not at all surprised. He'd already come to the same conclusion. They rounded up a workcrew and began. As one group of workers pried the sheets of roofing iron and planks of siding off the house, a chain of men moved the materials to the safety of the schoolhouse.

It took them a day to dismantle what had taken two months to build, but it had to be done. The building materials used to construct the house were too expensive to simply be abandoned and allowed to be swept away by the river.

The day after they dismantled the McCullys' new house, the rain stopped. This allowed Jim and Pete time to inspect the damage done by the river. The ground was so softened from the rain that during their inspection Jim's boots disappeared six inches into the mud with every step. Now that the rain had stopped and the swollen river was receding, Jim privately wondered whether they had done the right thing by pulling the house down.

Over the next several weeks, it continued to rain off and on, though not as heavy as before. And the ground was not drying out enough to allow reconstruction of the McCullys' house. Then on Thursday, July 30, Jim awoke to another deluge pelting the thatched roof of the hut. As little rivulets streamed down the window screens, Jim wondered whether the jungle would ever dry. Every piece of paper in the house was damp. Jim's boots grew a fresh batch of mold overnight, and Jim had been wearing the same musty-smelling clothes for over a week. Because of the rain nothing would dry.

After breakfast, Jim and Pete worked together on their Quichua dictionary. It was hard to concentrate, but there was nothing else they could do. It was just too wet to get anything done outside or to visit people in their huts.

When the two men broke at noon, Jim prepared lunch while Pete made a routine check outside the hut. Jim had just put a pot of water on the Coleman stove for coffee when Pete burst back into the living room. Pete yelled, "We've got to get out of here! The river's eating away under the bank. The house could be gone anytime."

Jim rushed outside to see for himself. As he did so, a massive mudslide fifteen feet from the hut plunged into the river with a whoosh. Pete was right, they had to get out—and fast.

Jim began to throw their kitchen things into a large bucket. Then he stopped and thought for a moment. Kitchen things weren't the most important things in the house; his language notes were. Jim grabbed a box and began emptying the contents of the living room bookshelf into it. Meanwhile, Pete was frantically throwing everything he could into boxes.

Suddenly, Jim stopped. The radio. They would have to dismantle the radio. Someone would have to climb up on the roof and retrieve the aerial. But was there time? And what would Marj Saint think when she tried to reach them and there was no reply? Jim dropped what he was holding and rushed for the transmitter. He needed to get a message out to Marj while he still could.

"Shandia to Shell Mera. Shandia to Shell Mera. Over," he called into the microphone, hoping Marj was nearby the radio in Shell Mera.

Finally, the radio crackled back, "I read you, Shandia. Shell Mera is standing by. Over."

Jim didn't have time to say much. "Marj, bad news. The river is eating away the bluff under the hut. We are only five yards from the edge now. I'll try to keep you posted, but if you don't hear from me at two o'clock, you'll know the house is over the edge. Over."

"Shell Mera reading you, Jim. Will pass the message along. God bless you, and be careful. Over and out."

While Jim was on the radio, Pete had been out in the torrential rain rounding up a team of helpers. None of the Indians lived as close to the edge of the bluff as the missionaries. And even if they would have to abandon their huts, it would take them only a few minutes to unhook their hammocks, collect their food baskets and spears, and flee. It wasn't that easy for the missionaries. Jim and Pete had been at Shandia almost a year and had gathered quite a collection of things.

The helpers formed a line from the house to the schoolhouse along which they passed Jim and Pete's belongings. The schoolhouse was still well back from the bluff's edge and seemed to be the safest place to store their goods.

Jim did his best to wrap the papers and books in plastic before handing them down the line, but he knew they were racing against time. Things did not get packed as well as he would have liked. He cringed when he saw some pages from his Quichua dictionary go toppling into the mud. One of the helpers quickly picked the mud-covered paper up and shoved it back into the box.

The McCullys had stored eleven barrels of clothes and household items in Jim and Pete's house. Jim laid each barrel on its side and rolled it to the top of the stairs, where he let it go. The Indian helpers then rolled the barrels into the jungle and stacked them. It was exhausting work, and by the time Jim and Pete started prying the split lengths of bamboo off the walls of their hut, the Indians had little energy left to carry the loads to safety. Despite their exhaustion, Jim and Pete had more work to do. Every item they lost now would have to be replaced later, costing both money and time.

"Get out! Get out!" the Indians suddenly yelled as they dropped the boards they were hauling and fled into the jungle. Jim, who had just unscrewed a cupboard from the wall, caught the panic in their voices. If men who had lived all their lives on this ground said it was time to leave, it was time to leave. Jim stuffed the screwdriver into his belt and bolted out the door. Whatever was left would have to be abandoned.

Jim kept running until he reached the edge of the clearing. He heard a massive thud behind him. He looked just in time to see his house roll slowly onto its side and disappear over the bluff into the raging river below.

"That won't be the end of it!" yelled Pete grimly from his perch on the schoolhouse roof. "I think we should get out of here. It might all go into the river."

"But what about the clinic?" asked Jim, unable to imagine abandoning their newest building to the swollen river.

"We don't have time!" Pete yelled back.

Jim had an idea. "It's not that big. How about we put a rope around it and drag it away from the edge. We could use some planks from our house as skids."

"It's too top heavy," Pete called back.

Jim was thinking fast. He hated to lose the new building, especially the thatched roof. With so many people living around Shandia, the special fronds used for roof thatch were in short supply. "We could tip the building on its side and drag the roof off it to safety," he suggested, uselessly wiping the rain out of his eyes with a sodden handkerchief.

"It's worth a try," Pete replied, "but we'd better move fast."

Within ten minutes, Jim had it organized. On the count of three, ten men pushed on the side of the clinic. The building toppled over, dangerously close to the edge of the bluff.

"I'll go around back and tie the rope to the roof," Jim told Pete.

Jim cautiously made his way around the toppled building. As he bent over and began tying the rope to the thatched roof, the ground around him groaned, then suddenly fell away into the river. Jim found himself balancing on a thin finger of earth that jutted out from under the building. He grabbed the rope to steady himself.

"He's dead!" yelled one of the Indians.

"No, I'm alive!" he called back and then instructed, "get me a machete!"

Jim held on desperately to the roof, his heart thumping audibly as he waited. At any moment that piece of ground he was balanced on could dive into the raging river, taking him with it. The building itself now balanced precariously on the edge of the bluff. Jim had no way to squeeze back around the clinic. His only escape route was through the roof.

After what seemed like an eternity, Jim heard a rustle and then saw the gleaming blade of a machete poking through the thatched roof. He grabbed it and pulled it all the way through, flipped it around, and grasped it by the handle.

Then, with frantic swings, he hacked a hole in the roof. As quickly as he could he clambered through the hole and along the wall of the overturned clinic to the door, through which he climbed to safety. As Jim emerged from the clinic building, a cheer went up from the Indians.

"Let's get out of here!" Jim yelled as he ran toward the jungle once again.

Somewhere along the way Jim's shoes slipped off in the gooey mud. Jim was vaguely aware they were gone, but he did not have the energy to reach down and pull them free. He continued on barefoot. About fifty yards farther, Jim reached the place where some of their belongings and the McCullys' barrels had been dumped. The whole scene reminded him of the aftermath of a tornado. Jim sat down heavily on one of the barrels, noticing with surprise that his feet were bleeding. Pete sank down beside him.

Ten minutes later a roar shook the jungle. It could mean only one thing: The clinic had gone over the edge. A chill ran down Jim's spine. What if more of the ground underneath them was being eaten away by the river? Jim looked around. He was surrounded by towering trees with huge roots that had been anchored there for a hundred years or more. Yet Jim had seen trees bigger than these tossed like twigs down the swollen river. As difficult as it was to face, he had a strong feeling they should move everything farther away from the hungry river.

Worse still, Jim began to fear for the schoolhouse and all the equipment and building materials now stored in it. He discussed his fears with Pete, who admitted he had the same fears. Jim and Pete asked the Indians to help them move all of their things another fifty yards into the jungle. As they began tearing apart the schoolhouse, Jim posted one of the Indians near the edge of the bluff to stand watch. He gave strict instructions for the man to yell as soon as it got too dangerous to keep stripping the school.

Six hours later, at three o'clock in the morning, all of their equipment and building materials were safely stowed far from the raging current. Jim and Pete gratefully accepted the invitation of one of their Indian helpers to stay in his hut for the night. Jim was asleep in seconds, more exhausted than he'd been in his entire life.

At 5:00 a.m. Jim was awakened by shouting. He pulled off the damp blanket he'd been sleeping under. As he tried to stand, he winced with pain from his swollen, cut feet. He hobbled outside to see what the frantic shouting was all about.

Pete awoke too, and followed Jim outside. The two men met Valencio, one of their helpers, who was running through the jungle at breakneck speed. "It's gone!" he yelled, breathing heavily and beckoning for the two missionaries to follow him.

Jim was wondering what was gone as he limped along behind Valencio. When the Indian stopped abruptly and pointed, Jim could see for himself what was gone. The land where the schoolhouse, playing field, and part of the airstrip had been was gone—swallowed by the river.

Jim turned away. He couldn't bear to look. A whole year's work had been washed away. He reached out and put his hand on Pete's shoulder. The two men stood in silence. There was nothing to say. The mission station at Shandia was no more.

Chapter 9

A New Direction

It continued to rain for two more days. There was nothing Jim and Pete could do but sit in the hospitable Quichua's hut and watch. Then, finally, the rain retreated. But as the sun came out, the jungle turned into a giant steam oven. Millions of gallons of water kept evaporating and condensing on the leaves of the tallest trees. Jim longed for the kind of crisp, dry sunshine that would dry their papers and clothing.

With the end of the rain came the job of figuring out what exactly had been saved from the flood and assessing the extent of the water damage. A quick count of the McCullys' barrels revealed that there were now only ten of the original eleven. Jim sighed. The missing barrel had probably been stolen. Jim had known there was such a risk, but there was nothing he could have done to prevent it. Rather than worry about what was missing, he decided to be grateful for all the things that had survived.

Jim's resolve to be grateful quickly evaporated when he noticed the wire for the radio aerial was missing. Jim distinctly remembered placing it near the top of the red box in which the radio had been stacked. Without the aerial, he wouldn't be able to call Shell Mera and update Marj Saint on the state of their circumstances.

Thanks to Betty, Jim had an alternative to fall back on in getting a message to the outside world, even if it was a lot slower. After hearing Jim's last radio message to Shell Mera, Betty had persuaded one of the Indians at Dos Rios to trek to Shandia and investigate how Jim was getting on. The man had arrived the night before with a letter for Jim and a loaf of Betty's homemade bread. Jim was amazed by the determination of his fiancée. He hadn't even considered sending a messenger out to Pano or Shell Mera with news, because he doubted he could find anyone willing to risk such a trek with the river in flood. Yet somehow, Betty had convinced someone to take a letter for her to Shandia.

Now the messenger could take a letter back to Betty and let her know the fate of Shandia. All Jim needed was a pen and some paper. He cast his eyes about the chaos that surrounded him. Where would he find a pen and a dry piece of paper? The items weren't easy to find, but finally, after hunting through several boxes, he managed to find a few usable sheets of paper. The paper was limp but not too wet to write on. He sat down under a tree and began to write. Holding nothing back, he told Betty everything that had happened. "Shandia is no more," he began. "The first house went about 3:30 p.m. on Thursday...."

The letter brought a swift response. Within twenty-four hours, Betty had trekked through the jungle to get to Jim. With her was a small band of Quichua Christians from Dos Rios. Once again, Betty surprised Jim with her determination and courage, and right away she set to work sorting and hanging things on bushes to dry. Jim was, of course, thrilled to have her with him, but he found it difficult to concentrate on her conversations. He kept drifting off. At first, he put it down to tiredness; he hadn't slept much in the past week. But even after a good night's sleep, he felt dizzy and vaguely out of touch with reality.

The next day, more help arrived. This time it was Dr. Tidmarsh and Nate Saint, who had flown to Pano, where they had left the plane and hiked the rest of the way. Dr. Tidmarsh took one look at Jim and ordered him to lie down. "Malaria," he said, shaking his head. "You must have caught it while you were moving your things to safety. You need complete bed rest."

For once, Jim did not argue. He climbed onto of a pile of bedding and lay down. Dr. Tidmarsh then unwrapped the strips of torn bedsheets Jim had bound around his feet. As he did so, Jim's mind drifted off, and for the next week Jim was in and out of consciousness.

In the meantime, Nate Saint returned to Shell Mera to collect Ed McCully, who had come down from Quito to survey the damage.

After a week of rest, Jim felt well enough to get up for short periods. During these times, he joined in discussions about what to do next.

Jim, Pete, and Ed McCully began to ask themselves some serious questions. Now that there was nothing left of Shandia, should they rebuild it in the same place? Was God perhaps trying to get their attention and lead them to a better place? Jim felt those questions could be answered only by traveling to other areas in Quichua territory and searching for more suitable sites. He and Pete had lived at Shandia for nearly a year, but because of all the building and language studies, neither of them had traveled far from the immediate area. Now that all their responsibilities had been swept away by the river, they had time to explore and see if God might be leading them somewhere new.

Betty waved from the bank of the river as the three men climbed into a dugout canoe with several Quichua Indians. The plan was to spend two or three weeks plying the waterways that crisscrossed Quichua territory and find a suitable location for a new mission station. Betty had agreed to stay behind in a tent and watch over their belongings.

Several days into the journey, they paddled down the Puyo River to the point where it met with the Pastaza River. At the junction of the two rivers, Jim spotted a group of huts. "Let's pull in here," he suggested.

An hour later, the three missionaries were squatting together outside one of the huts, talking to a small Quichua man who had introduced himself as Atanasio. The man didn't seem at all afraid of the three strangers and quite happily told them about his life. Atanasio explained that he lived in the hut with his two wives and fifteen children! Jim smiled. He'd already noticed several pairs of eyes staring shyly at them from behind the bushes.

Atanasio invited the group to stay for lunch. One of his wives spread a banana leaf in front of the guests and then loaded boiled manioc onto it from an aluminum pot that hung over the fire.

As they chewed away on the manioc, Atanasio looked directly at Jim and said more as a statement than a question, "You will come back? You will open a school for my children?"

"What did he say?" asked Ed McCully, who understood only a few words of Quichua.

"He's inviting us back. He wants us to start a school for his children!" said Jim.

The three men looked at each other. This was a rare invitation indeed. It normally took a long time to win the trust of Indians, and even longer to be invited to live among them. Could this be where God was leading them to set up a new mission station? It certainly seemed possible.

For the next week, the men thought and talked about the invitation as they paddled down the rivers. By the time they arrived back at Shandia, twenty-one days after setting out, they had a plan.

Jim took Betty aside to explain it to her. "As we see it, we've already invested a lot of work here in Shandia. The Indians know and trust us, and we shouldn't give that up. It makes sense for Ed and Marilou to move here, especially since they don't know the language yet and the Indians here are used to having a missionary around. Of course, Ed will need either Pete or me to stay with him, at least until he knows enough of the Quichua language to get by."

Betty nodded.

Jim continued. "We also think Atanasio's invitation is a sign from God that we should begin a station down there, too. It would take two people to start the station. The sensible thing would be for Pete to stay here with Ed and Marilou and for me to start the new station. But I'll need a partner. So…" Jim drew in a deep breath, "…how soon will you marry me?"

October 8, 1953, was Jim's twenty-sixth birthday. It was also his wedding day. Neither he nor Betty had wanted the usual wedding, with bridesmaids, cake, and bouquets of flowers. The ceremony was performed at the Registro Civil, an old colonial building in the heart of Quito. Dr. Tidmarsh, his wife, and Ed and Marilou McCully were the only witnesses. The whole event took less than ten minutes!

The new Mr. and Mrs. Elliot flew to Panama for their honeymoon and then on to Costa Rica, where they dropped in on Betty's brother Dave and his wife Phyl, who were missionaries there. Both Jim and Betty enjoyed surprising them. Dave and Phyl were certainly surprised—especially when they found out that Jim and Betty were married.

Once back in Quito, Jim and Betty directed their energy toward preparing to set up a new mission station at Puyupungu, as Atanasio's little clearing was called. Many of the supplies Jim had originally brought with him from the United States had never been unpacked. They hadn't yet been needed and so were still stored safely away at the Gospel Missionary Union compound in Quito.

Almost like opening wedding presents, the newlyweds rummaged through the collection of things looking for anything useful. They found several aluminum pans and containers, an assortment of garden tools, and a tiny portable stove, all of which would certainly be of use in setting up a new home. They packed the items carefully into boxes that had been lined with thick, waterproof paper.

Soon, all the arrangements had been made, and the young couple were on their way to their first home. Jim and Betty caught the bus to Shell Mera, where they stayed the night. The following morning, Nate Saint drove them to the end of the road that led in the direction of Puyupungu. The road ended abruptly at the river. They all piled out of the pickup, and Jim squinted into the morning sun, searching for the canoes he'd arranged to have meet them and take them downriver. A wave of relief swept over him when he spotted them waiting on the far side.

After the Indians had paddled across the river, the group began loading the Elliots' belongings into the canoes. A folding bed, a steel trunk, the boxes, and a tent were all expertly balanced in the center of the canoes. With a wave from Nate Saint, Jim, Betty, and their Indian friends were on their way down the muddy river.

About halfway to their destination, a group of Quichua Indians from Puyupungu had paddled upstream to meet them and escort them to their new home. As the canoes were pulled onto the beach, Jim smiled. Once again, he'd caught a glimpse of a small brown face eyeing him from the bushes. He squeezed Betty's hand and pointed to a little girl who quickly disappeared into the undergrowth.

Atanasio came out of his hut to meet Jim and Betty Elliot as though he were a king welcoming important people into his realm. He waved his hand toward a hut—a small bamboo structure with a thatched roof. "It is for you," he said grandly. Jim smiled and thanked him. With all the other things he and Betty had to do, it was a relief to know they wouldn't have to worry about housing.

An hour later, Jim and Betty's belongings were piled inside the quaint home. Atanasio's wives and some of the braver children took turns peeking through the doorway to see what was going on inside. Then something happened that Jim hadn't expected: gifts began to arrive. One Indian brought a bunch of plantains, another brought smoked fish wrapped in a banana leaf, and yet another carried in a pile of firewood and two papayas. The new couple now had their dinner, but more than that, they had a sign they were really welcome. They were among friends.

Everything seemed perfect as Jim and Betty went to bed that first night. The couple had plenty of food, friendly neighbors, and a roof over their heads. It was, however, the roof that proved to be a problem. For one thing, it was too low for these Americans to stand up straight under. After all, they were both about a foot taller than the average Indian. But they had expected that. What they hadn't expected was to be rained on by cockroaches. As the night progressed, hundreds of roaches dropped from the thatched roof onto the two of them. Jim could feel Betty shuddering beside him as she flicked the bugs off.

After a sleepless night, Jim and Betty decided to leave the hut to the roaches. They pitched their sixteen-foot-long tent nearby. The tent had no floor, and anything touching the sides got wet when it rained. But it was roach free! And not only that, the two of them could stand up in it.

Once they had arranged the tent, they were ready to begin their new life together at Puyupungu and face whatever the future held for them.

Chapter 10

Outstations

"Puyupungu to Shell Mera. Come in Shell Mera. Over." Jim was only vaguely aware of Betty at the radio, but he could make out anxiety in her voice. Betty repeated the message several times. Jim couldn't focus long enough to hear what else his wife was saying on the radio. His head hurt too much, and he didn't have the energy to open his eyes. He drifted from consciousness.

When he finally regained consciousness, Jim was surprised to learn that three weeks had passed since he'd gone to bed with a headache! Betty was sitting on a canvas campstool beside his bed. As she mopped his forehead with a damp cloth, she told him about the past three weeks. Jim's temperature had risen to 104 degrees Fahrenheit, and Betty had become concerned. After many frustrating attempts on the radio, she'd managed to get a weak connection to Marj Saint at Shell Mera. Even though Marj was a nurse, she hadn't been much help. Apart from recommending antimalaria drugs, which Betty was already giving him, she could not think of what the problem might be. It sounded like malaria, but she just wasn't sure. Jim was too sick to be moved to Shell Mera by canoe, and there was no airstrip anywhere nearby for a plane to land. Without further options, Betty had continued to pray for Jim.

As Betty had struggled alone to take care of her husband, she'd also had to contend with the thick mud that now made up the floor of the tent, not to mention the curious Quichuas, who came by every hour to ask her questions about Jim's illness that she had no answers to. Anxiously she had waited, not knowing whether Jim was going to live or die.

Another week passed before Jim felt strong enough to get out of bed. Wobbly at first, he took several more days to regain his strength. However, lying in bed had given Jim time to plan out the projects he intended to complete as soon as he was well enough. First he would build a schoolhouse and fulfill his promise to Atanasio. Then he would hack an airstrip from the jungle. His illness, whatever it had been, had reminded him how vital it was for him and Betty and Atanasio's family to have a quick way in and out of Puyupungu for emergencies.

Jim and Betty continued to learn the Quichua language. Jim had a substantial head start on Betty and was already able to hold interesting conversations with Atanasio and his family.

Although the Elliots were the only missionaries at Puyupungu, they never forgot that they were part of a pioneering team that included the McCullys and Pete Fleming. Each morning, they cranked up the radio to report in to Shell Mera and to hear news from the other missionaries in the area.

Jim and Betty were delighted to hear about the progress Pete was making rebuilding the McCullys' new home at Shandia. The roof was on, and Pete had just about finished cladding the walls. Although the house was not as big as the one they'd torn down during the flood, Pete was nonetheless proud of his workmanship, and he worked as fast as he could to finish the house. Besides wanting the McCullys to move down from Quito as soon as possible, Pete had another reason for finishing the house quickly. After the McCullys were settled in at Shandia, he planned to return to Seattle and marry his childhood sweetheart, Olive Ainslie. Jim and Betty's marriage had convinced Pete that there was a place for married missionary couples in the jungle of the Oriente.

By mid-December 1953, the McCullys were settled in their new house and Pete was making final preparations to return to the United States for several months. Since Jim and Betty were anxious to meet with everyone in Shandia before Pete left, they decided to visit Shandia for Christmas. However, a nine-hour trek along overgrown jungle trails lay between Puyupungu and the village of Puyo, where the road started and where they would meet Marj Saint. Marj had agreed to drive them to Shell Mera, where they would spend the night, and Nate Saint would fly them to Shandia the next morning.

Jim hired a young Quichua man to be their guide. Early on the morning of December 18, they set out. The trail was even more overgrown than they had been told. Jim and the guide had to stop frequently to hack away at vines and fallen branches. In the Amazon jungle, the Indians always make their trails on the highest ground so that the routes are still passable during the rainy season. Jim and Betty soon came to understand that this meant they would be climbing every hill on the way to Puyo rather than taking the low road around them.

As they marched in single file, Jim reminded Betty that they were on an adventure. They were probably the only white people to have walked this trail. With huge air plants dangling from the tops of the trees, some with leaves two or three feet wide, and with the constant backdrop of noise from monkeys, croaking tree frogs, and squawking parrots, it was easy to imagine they were back in prehistoric times. The exotic jungle surrounded them with natural beauty.

After five hours on the trail, the reality of the difficult journey began to sink in. Jim's back hurt from constantly bending over to climb under tree limbs. His hands were blistered from swinging the machete, and his feet hurt from the constant rubbing of his shoes.

Finally, when the dense jungle gave way to fields of sugarcane, Jim knew they must be close to Puyo. Sure enough, as they followed the path around the cane fields, they found Marj Saint waiting for them in a pickup truck.

Jim and Betty greeted Marj warmly. As usual, Marj had thought of everything. Cold drinks and thick slices of chocolate cake were waiting in a picnic basket. Nothing had tasted so good to the weary travelers in a long time.

Jim and Betty shared some of the cake with their guide, who then trotted off across the cane fields back towards Puyupungu. Jim swung their backpacks into the rear of the pickup, and the three of them were off to Shell Mera. It was certainly good to be riding instead of walking.

The next morning Jim and Betty arrived at Shandia, where they had a joyous reunion with the McCullys and Pete. Everyone had a lot of news to catch up on and a lot more planning to do. Pete and Ed told Jim about the growing interest in Christianity among the Indians around Shandia. Several of the Indians were taking part in regular Bible studies and were asking many questions. This excited Jim, who all along had thought that the role of a foreign missionary was to convert and train local people so that they could then reach out to members of their own tribe with the gospel message. Now it looked as though that strategy was becoming a possibility.

The missionaries talked about the best way to encourage this growing interest and decided to hold a Bible conference at Shandia after Christmas. Since by now Jim and Pete were able to speak fluent Quichua, the time seemed right to offer the Indians some in-depth Bible teaching.

Two days into the conference, Jim sat down to write to his parents. He sighed deeply as he wondered how to convey a sense of what it was like to host a series of Bible studies in the jungle. He thought about the meetings he'd attended every Sunday as a child in Portland. The children would all sit quietly beside their parents. Everyone would stand when it was time to sing a hymn and listen respectfully when one of the church elders got up to preach. Even if their minds were a thousand miles away, their bodies were still and quiet.

It was not that way among the Indians of the Oriente, however, who had no concept of being quiet, let alone reverent. The Indians even brought their pets to church with them! Monkeys perched restlessly on the heads of their owners, grooming themselves and reaching out to swat anything that came too close. Parrots, tethered to ropes, beat their wings and strutted up and down their owners' arms. Quichua women used church as a time to groom their children, picking lice from their hair, scraping their feet to pull out any protruding prickles or thorns, and cleaning their finger and toenails with twigs. The men would stand and stretch in the middle of the service, yell to passing people, or wander outside to use the "bathroom," which happened to be the outside wall of the church.

Jim tried to describe it to his parents. He had to admit to himself, though, that unless a person had experienced this behavior firsthand, it was hard to imagine just how distracting it could be.

Still, when the Bible conference was over, Jim was delighted to discover that some of the eighty or so Quichua Indians in attendance had been listening. Two of the teenage girls, Eugena and Carmela, asked to be baptized and after a question-and-answer time, it was obvious they understood fully what they were asking for. The next Sunday, Jim baptized the mission's first two Quichua converts in the Talac River.

The success of the Bible conference also led the missionaries to rethink their plans for the future. Jim had to admit that with the McCullys' house rebuilt and the airstrip repaired, Shandia was by far the best place for a central mission base. And with the growing interest the local Quichua Indians were showing in the gospel message, there was the potential to start a strong, thriving church that could eventually be taken over by the Indians themselves.

The more the missionaries talked, the more they began to think of Shandia as the hub of a wheel, with a number of smaller mission outposts spread along the rim. Since the goal was to train Quichua Indians to take the gospel message to others in their tribe, it seemed sensible to concentrate on an area where the multiplication strategy had the best chance of succeeding.

Before Jim and Betty left Shandia, they decided that Puyupungu should become a part-time mission station. Jim and Betty would return to their tent, and Jim would finish building a hut to serve as the permanent mission house. Then the couple would alternate several months at a time between running the school and a medical clinic in Puyupungu and living at Shandia.

As Jim and Betty trekked back to Puyupungu, they knew it was not going to be their long-term home. They expected, however, that it would take them a year or so to get everything established. They had no idea that in just a few short months they would be living in Shandia.

Just as he was putting the finishing touches on the new mission house, which featured screened windows and a roach-proof ceiling, Jim received a letter from his father in Portland, Oregon. His dad wanted to come down and help him with a building project.

Not having seen a single member of his family since waving good-bye to his parents in San Pedro two years before, Jim was obviously delighted, but one thing concerned him: His father wanted to help him build something, but there wasn't much more to build at Puyupungu. It made more sense for his dad to help with the rebuilding at Shandia. In May 1954, after school had been dismissed for the summer, Jim and Betty packed up their belongings, loaded them into dugout canoes, and paddled up the river to Shandia. A few days later, they flew out to Shell Mera to meet Mr. Elliot as he arrived on the bus from Quito. Jim and Betty had something exciting to tell him. He was going to be a grandpa! Betty was expecting their first baby, due early in the new year.

Mr. Elliot fit right in at Shandia. All his adult life he had been interested in missionary work and had tried to interest his children in it. Now he had his reward as he watched his son go about the work of being a missionary in the jungle of the Oriente.

Meanwhile, Ed McCully had been investigating other jungle locations that would make good outstations. He told Jim about a promising location called Arajuno. Until five years before, the well-known area had been a thriving Shell Oil exploration station, just like Shell Mera. Ed, who'd flown over the site several times with Nate Saint, reported that it was only a twelve-minute plane ride southeast of Shandia. Large numbers of Quichua Indians lived in the area. Arajuno even had a well-constructed, though overgrown, airstrip. There was just one catch: Shell Oil had abandoned Arajuno not because it had run out of oil but because of the Auca Indians.

Arajuno was situated right on the border of Auca territory, and the "neighbors" had been less than friendly. In 1947, three Shell employees, two Quichua Indians and one American, had been speared to death by Aucas. This had made it difficult for Shell to recruit more workers, but eventually Shell convinced enough Quichua Indians and foreigners that it was safe to return to oil prospecting. They were wrong. In 1948, eight Shell workers were speared to death in an ambush. After that, no one would work there, forcing Shell Oil to abandon the site altogether.

Now Arajuno was a ghost town. The tennis court was overrun with creepers, the hotel was tumbling down, and the bakery and general store had all but rotted away. The town had even had a narrow-gauge railway, on which a rusting steam engine still sat, a monument to a bustling past.

Should they pursue Arajuno as an outstation? For days, Jim and Ed wrestled with the difficult decision. They had not been invited by the local Indians to live there, as they had been in Puyupungu, and given their past history, the Auca Indians may well resent visitors. After much prayer, Jim and Ed felt they should begin making day trips to Arajuno to see what kind of response they would get from the local Quichua Indians.

Jim also began to pray that one day Arajuno might be a gateway through which the Auca Indians could be reached with the gospel message. The Aucas may have lived only forty miles away by air, but they were an eternity away in their understanding of God. Jim continually reassured himself that one day God would show him a way to reach these people.

Chapter 11

From the Air

ebruary 27, 1955, at Shell Mera, blonde-haired lerie Elliot was born. Her parents could not een more proud. Following the birth, Jim and tayed a week at Shell Mera. Jim spent his days g to build a medical clinic that would serve the naries of the Oriente. At lunchtime, he would back to the Saints' house to see how his wife ew baby were getting along.

etty and Marj Saint had a lot to talk about, cially since Marj also had a new baby son, p, born just two months before. Raising a baby ne Oriente had its own special challenges, and y was grateful for all the advice she could get.

In the evenings, with the crater of Mt. Sangay glowing red in the distance, Jim and Betty would sit at the table and talk with Nate and Marj Saint. Sometimes Johnny and Ruth Keenan, the new pilot and his wife who had come to help the Saints, would join them.

It was during these times that Jim relayed all that was happening at Shandia. Just weeks before, Jim, Pete, and Ed had held another Bible conference, which had been a great success. About one hundred Quichua Indians had attended. When the conference was over, four young men had asked to be baptized. Meanwhile, Marilou McCully had given birth in Quito to her second child, Michael. And Pete Fleming was now married to Olive. After spending time in Quito so that Olive could learn Spanish, the couple had returned to Shandia.

Inevitably, the conversation each night would turn to their neighbors, the Auca Indians. Nat knew more about them than anyone, since he an Marj had been at Shell Mera for seven years an had gathered many stories in that time. He sup posed there was some truth in each story, but th Aucas still remained elusive. And although th stories made Nate cautious about his safety as h flew near Auca territory, he fervently expressed h desire to communicate with the Aucas and sho them there was a better way to live than in an en less cycle of hatred and revenge. Jim seconded t motion.

The missionaries also discussed Arajuno. Na had agreed to help Ed McCully clear the aba doned airstrip there and find the best site on whi to build a house. Since no one wanted to take more risks than were absolutely necessary where the Auca Indians were concerned, Nate shared some good ideas on how to reduce the risks. Jim watched as Nate sketched plans for a battery-powered electric fence to skirt the perimeter of the property.

At the end of the week, Jim and Betty returned to Shandia with their new daughter. As Nate brought the Piper Cruiser to a halt at the end of the airstrip, the missionaries' Quichua friends ran out and surrounded the plane, crowding around Jim and Betty and the baby when they climbed out. They were fascinated with Valerie's fine blonde hair and tiny pink fingers. None of the Quichuas had ever seen a white baby before.

Once the Elliot and McCully babies were settled in their new routines, it was time for the adult team at Shandia to strategize. Should the McCullys move to Arajuno? Should someone move back to Puyupungu? The group faithfully prayed about these important questions before making any decisions.

As March progressed, the team agreed the McCullys should move to Arajuno. But a few days hence, the missionaries received a chilling reminder of how dangerous such a move would be. Another Auca attack took place close to Arajuno. This time, the Aucas had killed a mother and her two children and stolen their canoe.

The news did not dissuade the McCullys. They were sure Arajuno was where God was leading them, but they would take every precaution they could, including having Nate Saint set up his electric fence around the house.

Once the decision to move had been made, Ed and Nate quickly set about clearing the airstrip at Arajuno. As soon as they could land a plane there, the two men spent entire days in the abandoned settlement piecing together a house. Ed was hoping to open a school and a church there one day soon.

At about the same time, Pete and Olive Fleming decided they were ready to take up the challenge of moving to Puyupungu. The ministry model Jim had been working toward was finally starting to take shape. Jim and Betty would remain at Shandia, which would serve as the hub of the mission, while the McCullys would be at Arajuno to the southeast and the Flemings at Puyupungu to the south.

Life in the jungle was never dull. New challenges were always arising, as were new obstacles that had to be overcome. Jim was working hard translating the Gospel of Luke into the Quichua language as well as running school, church, and Bible classes. He also had to respond to countless medical emergencies. Sometimes he would hike for miles through the jungle to attend to an Indian who had been bitten by a snake or had broken a bone or had suffered any other type of injury. On occasion, he trekked through the jungle to retrieve a tool someone had "borrowed" from him while he wasn't looking. The garden Jim had planted needed constant attention. Weeds had to be pulled from among the beds of vegetables and flowers, and thousands of crawling and flying bugs had to be kept away from the tender plants.

Jim's passion for planting flowers was particularly puzzling to the Indians, who saw no reason to cultivate something that couldn't be eaten. The Indians would nudge each other and wonder aloud why anyone would put such energy into growing something as useless as flowers!

While Jim and Betty were busy in Shandia, the Flemings reopened the school at Puyupungu. Jim made regular trips there to encourage Pete and Olive and to visit with Atanasio.

In July, Jim's brother Bert and his wife Colleen came to visit from their mission station in Peru. The two brothers had a great time together and even managed a visit to Arajuno to see the McCullys. In Shandia, Bert witnessed the largest baptism held so far. Fourteen people were baptized at a small beach on the Talac River. It was a particularly satisfying baptismal service for Jim because the candidates had been discipled by some of the older Quichua Christians. The Quichua Christians were beginning to understand the need to take on the responsibility of the church themselves.

Jim had been particularly pleased when he interviewed Kupal Angu, one of the men wanting to be baptized. Everyone knew that Kupal Angu had had a violent argument with his wife a year before and had thrown her out of his hut. Kupal Angu's wife had not come back. The Quichua Christians had told Kupal Angu that he must make things right with her if he truly wanted to become a Christian and be baptized. At first, Kupal Angu refused, but then he finally gave in. As a result, he and his wife were reunited and baptized together.

Of course, the baptism was done Quichua style. As everyone gathered at the small beach to watch, the combined weight of three girls perched on a sandy bank caused the bank to give way. The girls came tumbling down onto the beach. Howls of laughter erupted from the crowd. Meanwhile, the boys took turns throwing stones into the river to see who could land his closest to Jim.

On September 29, not long after the baptism, Jim, Ed McCully, and two Indian helpers were scheduled to go to Villano to hold some meetings for a group of Quichuas who had not yet heard the gospel. The day before, Jim caught up with Ed in Arajuno, where Nate Saint was to rendezvous with them and fly them to their destination. Since there were too many of them for one flight, Nate was going to fly Jim and the equipment in first and then return to pick up Ed and the two Indian helpers.

Jim was anxious to get to Arajuno. Two weeks before, Ed and Nate Saint had spotted an Auca settlement from the air. Jim had not yet had a chance to ask Ed any questions about what they'd seen. He had been at Arajuno only a few minutes before he began peppering Ed with questions, and soon the story was tumbling out.

Nate Saint had been on his regular Monday morning grocery delivery flight to Arajuno when he had noticed it was an unusually clear day. He'd estimated he could see about seventy-five miles in any direction. As he touched down at Arajuno, Nate had had an idea. Why not take Ed up and look for the Aucas?

Ed had jumped at the idea, and half an hour later the two men were soaring over the jungle. Nate told Ed what to look for, but it was unlikely they would see the Aucas themselves; there were perhaps only five hundred to one thousand of them spread throughout the territory. What they needed to look for were areas of land that had been cleared of trees to grow manioc or wisps of telltale smoke curling up from a communal fire.

As Nate pointed the plane eastward, Ed looked intently out the window. About fifty miles from Arajuno, Ed thought he spotted an area that had once been a garden. Nate circled it in the plane, but neither of them was sure whether or not the treeless patch was manmade. The patch could have simply been the result of several old trees falling down.

The men flew on, and while Ed scoured the sea of trees below, Nate kept a close eye on the fuel gauge. Low on fuel, the men soon had to turn back. Just as Nate was calling it a day, he spotted a slight dip in the tree line about five miles away. With an anxious glance at the fuel gauge, he told Ed they would fly over and check it out before heading back to Arajuno. Both men kept their eyes fixed on the dip. The closer they got, the more excited they became. The dip was still there, only now it was a clearing—a cultivated clearing. They had found the Aucas!

Nate and Ed strained to take in the unique sight. Below them in a series of circles lay fifteen distinct clearings. But more exciting were the thatched-roof huts dotted among the clearings. The two missionaries strained as far forward as they could for a better view, but there were no Aucas in sight. Still, Nate and Ed had no doubt the village was being used by the Aucas.

As much as they wanted to stay and explore more, Nate could not risk staying over the area any longer. He switched to the reserve fuel tank and headed for Arajuno.

Ed's story of the Auca huts encouraged Jim. Now, on their way to Villano, a twenty-minute flight southeast from Arajuno, they would have to fly over Auca territory. Jim's heart raced at the thought of spotting the Aucas for himself. As soon as Nate took off, Jim pressed his face against the window, willing himself to see the elusive Aucas, or at least some sign of their presence in the jungle. Alas, he saw nothing. Disappointed, he climbed from the plane at Villano and unloaded his bags. Still, although Jim hadn't seen any Aucas, maybe Ed would on Nate's return trip with him.

Jim waited restlessly for the Piper Cruiser to return. Finally, he heard the buzz of an engine and then spotted the plane above the tree line. He ran to meet the yellow MAF plane carrying his friends.

Ed leapt out as soon as the plane came to a

stop, a huge grin lighting his face. "We found more Aucas," he announced jubilantly. "And this time, only fifteen minutes from Arajuno!"

A chill went down Jim's spine. Was God trying to tell them it was time to reach out to the Auca Indians? After all, Nate Saint had spent seven years flying over the jungle and had never once spotted them. Now, in just two weeks the Aucas had been spotted twice!

From the time he was a young boy sitting in a pew at the local Brethren assembly in Portland, Jim had considered missions. Now he was a missionary, and a unique and awesome challenge had been laid before him. The opportunity seemed to be opening up for him and his fellow missionaries to share the gospel message with a tribe of Indians who had survived alone in the dense jungle for thousands of years.

To Jim, it was as if every course he had studied in college, every church meeting he had attended, every Bible verse he had memorized was leading him toward this one great purpose of reaching the Auca Indians with the gospel message.

Chapter 12

A Plan Is Hatched

It was Sunday night, October 2, 1955, and four men were sprawled on the wooden floor of the Saints' living room in Shell Mera. Everyone was focused on a map of the Oriente and, in particular, an area directly east of Arajuno—Auca territory.

Some might have said it was a coincidence that the men were there together, but not Jim Elliot. Jim held a strong conviction that God's hand had moved to bring the men in that room together at this time.

Johnny Keenan had been flying Jim and Ed back to Arajuno from Villano when a fierce storm blew up out of nowhere. To avoid the storm, Johnny had been forced to divert to Shell Mera. When the storm didn't let up, there was nothing else to do but spend the night at Shell Mera and hope that the weather would be suitable for flying in the morning.

And now, here they were—Jim Elliot, Ed McCully, Nate Saint, and Johnny Keenan—intently studying a map of the Oriente and hoping to find some clue about what to do next.

All of them agreed that the pace of "Operation Auca," as they had dubbed it, was picking up speed. Not only had there been two sightings of Auca settlements in the past two weeks, but other things were falling into place as well. With Johnny Keenan to share the workload, Nate Saint had time to help plan for, and even take part in, a face-to-face meeting with the Aucas. Similarly, Jim's work at Shandia was moving ahead quickly. There was now a nucleus of twenty-five Quichua Christians in the church, and some of them showed considerable promise as leaders. This freed Jim to concentrate on other things.

At the same time as things were moving ahead in Shandia, Ed and Marilou had been accepted by the Quichua Indians at Arajuno. Although several of the Indians claimed to have seen Auca footprints around the outside of the McCullys' electric fence, there had been no attacks. And now that an Auca settlement had been found just fifteen minutes away by air, Arajuno would make a great starting point for an expedition into Auca territory.

Many challenges were yet to be overcome if Operation Auca was to move ahead. While finding the Auca settlements had been a positive first step, the eager missionaries still didn't know how to convince the Aucas that they were friendly and meant them no harm. That was going to be difficult. If the Aucas spoke the Quichua language, the whole process would be much easier, but they didn't. They spoke their own language—one that didn't sound anything like the language of their Indian neighbors.

As the men contemplated the challenge before them, Nate Saint reminded Jim of something. Nate's sister Rachel, a missionary with Wycliffe Bible Translators, was working to gain an understanding of the Auca language from an Auca woman named Dayuma, who had left her tribe a number of years before. Dayuma lived at Hacienda Ila, a large plantation south of Shandia.

Jim nodded. He recalled hearing about this Auca woman from some of the Quichua girls at Shandia. The girls had said that Dayuma had the long earlobes of an Auca, but she no longer plugged them with balsa earrings. Instead, she dressed and acted more like a Quichua.

"Is Rachel at Hacienda Ila right now?" Jim asked Nate.

"No," Nate replied, "she's at a conference in Quito for a couple of weeks."

Jim breathed a sigh of relief. As much as he would have liked to involve Rachel in their operation, the men had already agreed not to tell their plans to any more people than was absolutely necessary. Many of the other Indian tribes in the Oriente, not to mention the Ecuadorian military, would have loved to know the Aucas' location so they could strike back at them. Since it seemed that most people would rather see the Aucas dead than alive, the Aucas' whereabouts could not leak out. Operation Auca would have to remain a secret.

Since Hacienda Ila was only a four-hour trek from Shandia, Jim offered to walk there, visit Dayuma, and find out what he could about the Auca language from her. He promised he would be careful not to raise her suspicions.

The group also considered how they could prepare the Aucas to meet them. As they discussed their ideas, Nate Saint described a technique he had developed called the *spiral-line drop* for lowering things to the ground from his airplane. Nate would fly his plane in a tight circle over a particular spot and then lower a canvas bucket on the end of a long length of rope. As the bucket was dropped toward the ground, the rope would form a spiral. The bucket would then hang steady in the middle of the spiral, as though it were in the eye of a hurricane. Using this ingenious technique, when there was no airstrip nearby to land, Nate had been able to deliver items to missionaries on the ground and receive items back. The technique was also a lot more accurate than just dropping things from his plane and hoping they landed in the right place. More often than not, "bombing" an area didn't put things where they should go, and a missionary would sometimes have to scamper up a tree to retrieve supplies. The spiral-line drop had proven invaluable in emergencies. On several occasions, when the person on the ground had no radio, Nate had dropped a telephone in the bucket so they could communicate directly.

Now the spiral-line drop could be put to a whole new use. Nate could use it to send gifts of friendship to the Stone Age Auca Indians.

Jim thought it was a great idea. The men could make contact with the Aucas without putting themselves in danger. But there was still a problem to solve: the spiral-line system relied on the person on the ground retrieving the goods directly from the bucket. Jim wasn't so sure the Aucas would do that, at least not right away.

The men puzzled over the problem as they drank some hot chocolate. Nate decided that what they needed was an automatic release that would detach the bucket and leave it behind on the ground with the gifts in it. Then, after the airplane had left, the Aucas could safely retrieve the gifts. Nate agreed to design an automatic release mechanism.

Next was the question of what to put in the bucket. The men had lots of ideas, some serious, some silly. They narrowed the list of likely gifts to smoked meat, cheese, salt, candy, cooking implements, paring knives, aluminum pots, plastic containers, and machetes (the one Western item the Indians prized above all).

The following morning, the weather had improved. Nate flew Ed to Arajuno and then took Jim on to Shandia.

A week after returning to Shandia, Jim made the trek to Hacienda Ila. Arriving around noon, he was invited to lunch with the plantation owner, Señor don Carlos Sevilla. At lunch, when Jim asked Señor Sevilla if he could spend some time with Dayuma, Señor Sevilla agreed without asking any questions. Since Rachel Saint spent so much time with Dayuma, he assumed all missionaries were interested in meeting the girl.

Jim sat on a low stool and stared at the Auca woman close up. Dayuma was short and dark, with high cheekbones. She looked remarkably like a Quichua Indian, except for the telltale earlobes. Jim had been told that both Auca men and women had their ears pierced at a young age and tiny balsa wood earplugs were inserted into the opening. As the child got older, the hole in the ear was stretched with larger and larger earplugs, until by the time the child was a teenager the hole was the size of a silver dollar.

Dayuma seemed eager to help. Jim decided it was probably because she was being excused from digging manioc or doing some other menial task. Dayuma didn't ask a lot of questions either. She just seemed content to answer Jim's inquiries.

Before long, Jim had his little black notebook out, jotting down the simple Auca words and phrases Dayuma was giving him. By the end of an hour, Jim had compiled a respectable vocabulary to study. He thanked Dayuma and asked Señor Sevilla if he could visit again.

"You're welcome anytime, as long as you stay for lunch and make good conversation," laughed Señor Sevilla.

As Jim trekked back through the jungle, he repeated several Auca sentences to himself. "*Bito weka pomopa*" and "*Abomiro imi?*" He thought the phrases had a singsong quality to them, making them easy to remember. The first phrase meant "I want to come near you," and the second meant "What is your name?" Both were good phrases for demonstrating to someone that you wanted to be his friend, especially when friendship was a matter of life or death!

Over the next month, the men involved in Operation Auca kept in contact with each other through coded radio messages and through letters sent with Nate Saint on the weekly vegetable run. Jim also made a trip to Puyupungu to update Pete Fleming on all the details of the operation.

Jim visited Dayuma several more times and soon had a stack of index cards with an Auca word or phrase written on one side and the English equivalent on the other. Although the phrases were only pebbles in comparison to the mountain that is the entire Auca language, Jim knew that overcoming the language barrier was critical to helping the Aucas understand that the missionaries came as friends. His hope was that the few Auca words and phrases they had learned would open the door to communication with the Aucas.

Meanwhile, Nate Saint and Johnny Keenan were busy working on a way to release the bucket from the rope once it hit the ground. The solution proved to be simple but effective. It consisted of a broom handle and two loops of rope. One loop was attached to the end of the rope, and the other to the bucket. When the bucket hit the ground, the tension on the rope was released and the loop that was attached to the bucket slipped off the broom handle. When the rope was reeled back in, the bucket was left behind on the ground.

On October 6, 1955, Jim waited anxiously by the radio. If the weather was clear at Shell Mera, Nate Saint and Ed McCully planned to drop the first gifts to the Aucas. Finally, the radio crackled. Marj Saint was reporting the good news that the yellow Piper Cruiser was headed toward Auca territory. Jim and Betty prayed diligently for Nate and Ed while waiting to hear further.

Several hours later, Nate's voice came over the radio with more good news. The gift drop had been a success. Somewhere in the jungle southeast of Arajuno, a group of Auca Indians were now dividing up the gifts. The plane had lowered a bucket containing a metal kettle with a lid, a bag of salt, some brightly colored buttons (raided from Marj Saint's sewing box), and a dozen or so yards of brightly colored ribbon (also from the sewing box). Even though Nate didn't report actually seeing any Aucas, he and Ed felt confident that many pairs of eyes had been watching the drop from among the trees of the surrounding jungle.

After the second drop, a week later, there was even better news: Nate and Ed had seen the Aucas! While circling about 2,500 feet above the settlement, Ed saw a single Auca man directly beneath the plane. The man was running backward and forward, although he did not appear to be attempting to scurry out of view. Within seconds, he was joined by two other Auca men, and the three of them ran around together. Ed pointed to them while Nate craned to see them over the instrument panel.

The two missionaries had decided that this was the right place to make the gift drop, and when Nate signaled, Ed began to let out the rope to lower the bucket. The men had placed in the bucket a machete wrapped in heavy canvas so that no one on the ground would reach for it and cut himself. When the bucket had nearly reached the ground, the machete fell out and tumbled into a stream. One of the Auca men dived in to claim it. Four other men emerged from the jungle, and soon all of them were gathered around admiring the machete.

Now that the missionaries had actually seen the Aucas, they decided that each member of the Operation Auca team would take a turn flying with Nate on the gift drops. Jim was thrilled. He was scheduled to go with Nate on the next trip.

Interestingly, it seemed that the Aucas were as fascinated with the missionaries as the missionaries were with the Aucas. Several more Quichua Indians had reported seeing Auca footprints near the McCullys' Arajuno house. Jim and the others agreed that the McCullys were probably being watched most of the time, and they wondered what to do about it. They hoped the Aucas connected the house with the gift drops, but there was no way to be sure. What was needed was a way to help the Aucas make the connection. Eventually, the missionaries hung a large model airplane from the McCullys' roof along with photos of each of the men. Then the Aucas would be able to understand that the house, the airplane, the gifts, and the missionaries were all linked together.

The next gift drop was on the first Thursday in November. Jim waited in great anticipation beside the airstrip at Shandia, straining to hear the Piper Cruiser's engine. Soon, he heard its familiar revving buzz, and in no time Nate Saint had pulled the plane to a halt at the end of the airstrip.

"Did you get it finished?" Jim asked Nate as he climbed into the airplane and buckled his seat belt.

"Sure did," replied Nate with a grin, patting a large box behind him. "Here it is. The loudspeaker's all hooked up and ready to go. Are you ready with the phrases?"

Now it was Jim's turn to grin. "Ready? I've been ready for this all my life."

As the Piper gained altitude and banked away from Shandia, Jim unsuccessfully tried to calm himself down. He was on his way to converse with the Aucas, a thrilling proposition, even though he knew it wouldn't be a real conversation. Twenty minutes later, the plane was nearing the Auca settlement.

Nate pointed toward the ground, and Jim peered from the plane to catch his first glimpse of the Aucas.

"I see their huts!" he yelled to Nate, expecting an Auca to emerge from one at any moment.

No Aucas appeared.

"I don't see any people yet," Jim informed Nate.

"You may not see them now, but just wait until we drop the bucket. If past behavior is anything to go by, they'll come running once they see it. First though, I'll make a couple of low passes so you can try out this gadget."

Nate descended until he was about five hundred feet above the settlement. Jim again peered from the plane, fascinated. Below him he could clearly see the tops of rectangular thatched houses, with canoes pulled up on the riverbank in front of the houses.

Finally, the time had come. With trembling hands, Jim picked up the microphone. Holding it close to his lips, he said, "*Bito weka pomopa.*"

Nate and Jim made a couple of passes over the settlement, with Jim using the loudspeaker to speak his phrases to the Aucas. Then Nate pulled on the yoke, and the Piper began to climb. When they got back to 2,500 feet in altitude, Nate gave Jim instructions on how to lower the bucket of gifts.

Sure enough, once Jim lowered the bucket to the ground, a group of Auca men descended upon it from the jungle like ants on an apple core. Nate did not even have to use the automatic release system anymore; the Aucas came right to the bucket while it was still attached to the rope.

"I see them!" yelled Jim. "I see them!"

Jim watched the drama unfold below. The Auca villager who had won the grab for the machete in the bucket held it high over his head and whirled it around. The blade glistened in the sun. Then the man cupped his hands and seemed to shout something at the plane.

"I think he's saying thank you," Jim yelled excitedly to Nate. "Let's try something else."

"Sure. There's an aluminum pot behind your seat."

Jim reeled the bucket back into the plane. He reached behind his seat and lifted the pot, opened its lid, and looked inside. The pot contained bunches of ribbons, a yellow shirt, and a string of beads. Jim placed it in the bucket, and the gift-drop procedure began again. This time, the Aucas stayed in sight while the bucket was lowered. The eager group grabbed it and emptied its contents before it even touched the ground.

Nate banked the plane to the northwest. It was time to head home. First stop was Arajuno, where Ed was waiting at the airstrip for them.

The three men walked to the house, where Marilou produced a tray of cookies and a pitcher of lemonade. As they enjoyed their snack, the men got into a serious discussion about their next step. Jim suggested they should enter Auca territory during the first full moon of the new year, which was to be on January 3, 1956. The light of the full moon would help to spot anyone creeping up on them during the night. The team would paddle down the river in canoes until they found a suitable piece of land on which to clear an airstrip. That way, they could land the airplane, and the Aucas would surely recognize it. There would be no mistaking the fact that these were the same men who had been shouting friendly greetings from above and dropping gifts to them.

Not everyone agreed with Jim's idea. Ed McCully wanted Jim to learn more of the language before they tried face-to-face contact. He knew that pronouncing just one word incorrectly could put them all in danger. Nate Saint, on the other hand, thought they should continue with the gift drops and wait and see what became of that. Besides, the rainy season started in mid-January, making it virtually impossible to clear land for an airstrip. He suggested they wait until the start of the next dry season. And anyway, the Aucas obviously knew where the McCullys lived. Perhaps if everyone was patient, the Aucas would come to them.

The men might have disagreed on the details of when and how a meeting should take place, but they were united on two things. First, they were committed to reaching the Aucas with the gospel message; and second, Operation Auca was going much better than anyone had expected. Apart from that, they would have plenty of time to hammer out the details of their first meeting with the Aucas, or so they thought.

Chapter 13

A Place to Land

Jim turned the headband over in his hands. It was a work of art. A line of fluffy, lime green parrot feathers was woven all the way around the headband. Sticking out from among the parrot feathers, on what Jim assumed to be the front of the headband, were longer feathers the color of nearly ripe tomatoes, like the ones growing in Jim's garden. "Come in and have something to drink and tell me all about it," Jim said to Ed McCully and Nate Saint, who were standing beside him on the airstrip at Shandia.

As they strolled into the house, Ed and Nate began telling Jim the story of how they received the headband. There wasn't much to tell, really. During their regularly scheduled gift drop, an Auca man had removed the clothes and enamel bowl from the bucket and then put something in it to be transported back to the airplane. When Ed had finally pulled the bucket into the circling Piper, there was the headband.

"It's obviously a gift," said Ed.

"Looks like they want to be our friends. This is great. One of us can wear the headband when we go to meet them. That way, they'll know we're the ones who give them gifts from the sky," said Jim excitedly.

"Great idea," Ed said enthusiastically. "I can't believe how fast this is all coming together."

Nate and Jim nodded.

The three men sat around the Elliots' dining table for half an hour, eating chunks of pineapple and papaya, drinking lemonade, and discussing how the headband was one more sign they were on track with Operation Auca. The time for a face-to-face meeting must be getting close.

All too soon, it was time for Nate and Ed to leave. They climbed back into the Piper Cruiser and took off for Arajuno. As the plane disappeared, Jim looked forward to the following week when it was his turn to go with Nate on the gift drop.

The week dragged, but finally Thursday rolled around. It was a clear but slightly windy day. Jim and Nate flew first to Arajuno, where they prepared the plane for the gift drop. Jim stowed the canvas bucket and rope behind his seat. Nate loaded a box containing the gifts they were going to dispense that day. As they worked, two Quichua Indians walked by. They stopped and took a long look at what the two missionaries were doing. "You missionaries are crazy. You give all the best stuff to the Aucas. Why don't you give it to us?" they said.

Jim's heart skipped a beat. The Indians had said it jokingly, but it set off an alarm bell in Jim's mind. The secret was out! Did all the Quichua Indians in the area know the missionaries were dropping gifts to the Aucas? Jim turned to Nate and asked, "What do we do now?"

Nate had no answer, but Jim knew it was something they would have to think seriously about. If the Quichua Indians managed to pinpoint exactly where the Aucas lived, a war could break out.

Once in the air and soaring over the tangled jungle, Jim's thoughts turned to the gift drop. Today, they were going to try something different. Jim and Nate were going to attempt to show the Aucas that several large trees needed to be cut down in preparation for an airstrip inside Auca territory. Jim had not learned enough of the language to be able to tell the villagers directly, so another plan had been formed to get the message across. The gifts were going to be dropped on top of the trees that needed to be cut down in the hopes that the Aucas would want the gifts enough to cut down the trees to retrieve them. No one was sure the plan would work, but it was worth a try.

"We should spot them any minute now," Nate called over the sound of the engine as the plane approached a clearing that contained several Auca huts. Nate looped the Piper over the clearing a couple of times, flying low enough for the Aucas to clearly see the two missionaries inside. This was part of the plan. When the two groups finally met face-to-face, the missionaries wanted the Aucas to be able to recognize them as the same men who had been giving them the gifts.

"There they are—two of them!" yelled Jim.

Nate dipped the wing a few degrees to see and then nodded. The plane turned sharply into the wind. "Are you ready with the first drop?" he asked Jim.

Jim held up an ax wrapped in canvas cloth. "Tell me when to drop it."

Nate slowed the Piper as much as possible and aimed for the largest tree at the edge of the clearing. "Now!" he yelled to Jim.

Jim let go of the ax. As it tumbled down, he hoped that it would get caught up in the high branches of the tree. Instead, the ax plummeted all the way to the ground and landed beside the tree. Two young Auca men raced over to get it.

Nate shook his head in disappointment. "Let's try it again. I'll come around for another pass."

This time, the bundle—four plastic combs wrapped in cotton bandages— landed gracefully on a branch near the top of the tree. The Auca men looked puzzled.

"I hope they want the stuff enough to cut the tree down to get it," said Jim.

"We'll find out next week, I guess," replied Nate with a hint of doubt in his voice.

As Nate looped the plane around and flew back over the clearing, Jim spotted an old man dancing around and waving his arms up and down. "Looks like he's inviting us down to visit," he blurted excitedly to Nate, the hair on the back of his neck standing on end.

Nate nodded.

"They look so friendly. I think they would welcome us," Jim went on. In the back of his mind, though, another voice was speaking, the voice of Dayuma. Jim mulled over what she had told him during their last visit. "Never, ever trust them," she had said. "You might think you know what they're going to do next, but you don't. Never, ever trust them!"

Jim tried not to listen too closely to the negative voice. If they did not trust the Aucas at some point, how would they ever be able to meet with them face-to-face and share the gospel? Yet Jim could not let Dayuma's warning go unheeded. Meeting the Aucas was going to require a balance of trust and caution on the missionaries' part.

"How about dropping them a pair of trousers?" Nate Saint's voice interrupted Jim's thoughts.

"Sure," said Jim, reaching behind him for a bundle of clothes. "Do you want me to drop it near the small house?"

"I think so," replied Nate.

Jim dropped the bundle from the plane and watched as the old man scrambled to get it.

"Let's try one more gift," said Nate.

Jim nodded in agreement.

"The wind's a bit stronger than normal, and out of the northwest too, but let's try a bucket drop anyway. There's a pot back there we can put in it."

Soon Jim had the pot in the canvas bucket and was ready to lower the gift to the ground. He waited for Nate to get the Piper flying in a tight circle above the clearing.

"Try to land it on the edge of the river," Nate told him.

Easier said than done. With the crosswind, it was almost impossible to direct the bucket anywhere. Finally, after seven attempts, Jim guided the bucket to rest on the edge of the small river that flowed alongside the clearing. The bucket was immediately swarmed by five young Auca men.

"They've got it!" said Jim triumphantly.

The plane continued to circle as one of the Indians removed the pot. "They're sending something up to us!" Jim yelled to Nate.

"Great. Let me level off and slow the plane a bit, and then you can pull it in."

"What a way to end the visit!" exclaimed Jim, hardly able to wait for what the Aucas were sending up.

As Nate began to level the plane, the radio crackled. "56 Henry, come in. This is Shell Mera. Over."

It was the voice of Marj Saint. Nate reached for the microphone. "Shell Mera, this is 56 Henry. Go ahead. Over." 56 Henry was the call sign for Nate's Piper Cruiser.

"Nate, Frank Drown's baby at Macuma is sick and needs to be flown immediately to the clinic at Shell Mera. Over."

"I read you. I'll head there right away. Let them know I should be there in about thirty-five minutes. Over."

"Will do. This is Shell Mera, over and out." Marj's voice faded from the crackling radio.

"Sorry about this, but I don't have time to drop you off. You'll have to come with me," Nate said to Jim as he pulled the throttle to the full-power position.

The Piper immediately began to gather speed. Jim felt the wind pulling at the bucket, which was still dangling from the end of the rope.

"You'll have to pull the bucket in as best you can. I don't have time to slow down while you do it," Nate told him.

Jim nodded that he understood. If Valerie was sick, he would want Nate to get to Shandia as quickly as possible. He began to reel in the rope. It wasn't easy, though. The wind resistance on the bucket meant he had to strain every inch of the way to get the bucket back into the plane. To his great disappointment, when he finally reeled it in, the gift the Aucas had placed in it was gone. It had been blown out by the wind. Jim wondered the rest of the way to Macuma, and then on to Shell Mera from there, what the gift had been.

The gift drops continued regularly every Thursday. Regrettably, the Aucas didn't seem to get the message about cutting down the trees to open up a possible landing strip. They managed to retrieve the gifts from the top of the trees without ever swinging a blade.

In mid-December, Nate Saint made a discovery that got everyone excited. He and Ed McCully had finished the scheduled gift drop and were on the way back to Arajuno when they decided to fly along the Curaray River, which ran through Auca territory. As they followed the river, Nate spotted a stretch of white sandy beach alongside it. He and Ed made a return flight a few days later to investigate the beach a little closer. They flew in low, and while Nate kept the Piper level at a steady sixty miles per hour, Ed dropped small paper bags of flour at two-second intervals. From the number of bags that hit the beach, Nate and Ed were able to estimate that the stretch of sand was two hundred ten yards in length—just long enough to land the plane. They nicknamed the sandy stretch "Palm Beach."

Nate told Jim that in all his years of flying over the Oriente, he had never seen a beach that was so long or straight. There was just one problem–the beach probably wouldn't be there for long. The tributaries of the mighty Amazon River changed constantly, building up a sand bank on one side of the river while carrying another away. If they were going to use Palm Beach as a landing site for a face-to-face meeting with the Aucas, they were going to have to do it soon. Otherwise, the rainy season of mid-January would most likely destroy their new airstrip.

With that realization, plans for the next stage of Operation Auca went into high gear. The men decided to follow the schedule Jim had been suggesting all along. On January 3, the next full moon, and the last full moon before the wet season set in, the anxious missionaries would land on Palm Beach and attempt to make contact with the Auca Indians. If the Aucas didn't come the first day, the men would camp out on the beach until they arrived. This strategy was likely to be less threatening than just walking into an Auca settlement. One thing they knew for sure: do not surprise an Auca warrior!

The next piece of the puzzle was where exactly to stay on the beach. A tent seemed too flimsy. A spear could be thrust right through it without any warning, and it would take all four men to stand guard at night, meaning no one would get any sleep. Jim came up with a better idea. As a boy back in Portland, he and his friends had built countless tree houses during summer vacations. Why not build a tree house in one of the ironwood trees that stood on the far edge of the beach? From up in a tree house they would be able to see anyone coming, and it would be hard for anyone to sneak up on them during the night. Everyone agreed it was a good idea. Since he had the most construction experience, Jim was given the job of cutting all the necessary timber. By transporting precut pieces of wood, the men could more quickly build the tree house once they unloaded on Palm Beach. They could not afford to be stranded out in the open for even one night.

The time came to make a solid commitment to Operation Auca. Jim, Ed, and Nate were fully committed to an up-close and personal meeting with the Auca Indians. Pete Fleming supported the idea, but he wasn't sure he felt called to go with the others. In case Pete decided not to go, the others decided to recruit a backup person for the team. But who?

Because Nate flew to nearly all the mission stations across the Oriente, he knew better than anyone most of the missionaries in the area. Roger Youderian came immediately to Nate's mind. Roger was a rugged, outdoors type. He had been a paratrooper in Europe during World War II, been decorated for action in the Battle of the Bulge, and survived the American assault at the Rhine in 1944. Originally from Montana, Roger and his wife Barbara had been missionaries for three years with Gospel Missionary Union at Macuma. They worked alongside Frank and Marie Drown, sharing the gospel message with the Jivaro Indians—a tough assignment. Until very recently, the Jivaros had been a tribe with a special reputation. They were the only people in the Amazon who were known to cut off their enemies' heads and shrink them. When the heads had been shrunk to the size of a baseball, the Jivaros wore them for decoration, hanging them from their waistbands. If there was to be another man on the team, Nate could think of no one more suitable than Roger Youderian.

Although Jim, Ed, and Pete knew of Roger, they didn't know him personally. So they took Nate's word that he was the right man for the job. Within a few days, Nate had talked to Roger about Operation Auca, and Roger had agreed to be part of the team.

On December 24, 1955, Jim, Betty, and ten-month-old Valerie, along with Pete and Olive Fleming, joined Ed and Marilou McCully and their two sons, Stevie and Mike, at Arajuno for Christmas. A sense of anticipation filled the air. Events were quickly unfolding.

Jim was particularly struck by an encounter that Marilou McCully had had only two days before the Elliots and the Flemings arrived. Marilou poured out the details the first night everyone was together.

On Friday, Marilou was awakened at five-thirty by a Quichua Indian named Fermin, who was staying in the little schoolhouse within the Arajuno compound to guard the house while Ed was away overnight holding an evangelistic meeting at Puyupungu with Pete Fleming. Fermin was yelling outside her window, saying something about needing ammunition quickly. Marilou threw on some clothes and ran to see what Fermin was yelling about. She managed to calm him down enough for him to tell her he had seen an Auca warrior carrying a spear no more than fifty yards from the house, just outside the electric fence. Fermin begged Marilou for ammunition for the gun so he could chase after the Auca and shoot him.

Marilou had another idea. She took the gun away from Fermin and grabbed a machete. Seven months pregnant, she walked toward the electric fence perimeter, holding the machete above her head and yelling at the top of her lungs, *"Bito weka pomopa!"* (I want to come near you).

At the same time, Fermin was yelling after her in Quichua, "You're crazy, lady. They'll kill you. Come back!" He was panicking because he did not have the gun to protect her. But Marilou did not turn back. Instead, her eyes eagerly searched the jungle. If the Auca warrior had come to pay her a visit, she wanted him to know he was welcome. However, the Auca had already blended back into the dark undergrowth.

Jim and Betty and the others talked for a long time about the possible significance of the event. Did it mean their neighbors were becoming more friendly? Was it a sign the Aucas were ready to meet with the missionaries? The group decided it was, and plans for the next phase of Operation Auca sped into their final stage.

Almost the entire Christmas holiday was taken up with Operation Auca. Jim taught Ed and Pete several more Auca phrases so they would be able to speak a few friendly words when they finally met the Aucas face-to-face. The men also plotted exactly what they would do once they landed on Palm Beach. Jim had made good progress on cutting the wood for the tree house. Once Nate Saint had ferried the timber in, the men would hoist it up into one of the tall ironwood trees and assemble the tree house. Before sunset each day, Nate Saint would fly back to Arajuno and stay there overnight, keeping the airplane out of danger from both the unpredictable river and Auca spears.

The other men would spend the night in the tree house. In the morning, they would climb down and yell Auca phrases into the jungle while Nate flew over "Terminal City," the name given to the Auca settlement where the missionaries had conducted the gift drops. Using the loudspeaker, Nate would broadcast in the Auca language, "Come to the Curaray. We want to meet you." He would then fly to Palm Beach and land. Then all the missionaries would wait to see what happened.

The men repeatedly went over every aspect of their plan, looking for flaws and examining every possible contingency. By the time Jim returned to Shandia the day after Christmas, he was sure of two things: one, it was God's timing to visit the Auca now; and two, they had taken every possible precaution. Jim hoped and prayed with the others that the final phase of Operation Auca would be a success.

Chapter 14

Operation Auca

In Shandia, there was plenty to do. Jim's garden, which had been so hard to establish, was now thriving. He was proud to be able to supply his family with homegrown squash and tomatoes. And the white gladioli bulbs his mother had sent him the year before were now standing tall and in full bloom. Tiny bushes of Mexican peppers dotted the garden, and the smell of citrus trees sweetened the air.

Valerie was growing even faster than the garden. She was now eleven months old and already pulling herself up on the furniture and standing on her wobbly legs.

The church was also thriving. On New Year's Day, Jim finished hosting another Bible conference. As in years past, it was a great success.

The following morning, January 2, Jim waited anxiously by the radio for news. Finally, he heard what he'd been waiting for. According to Nate Saint, everything was in place for visiting their neighbors. Nate was flying in at lunchtime to pick Jim up and take him to Arajuno to prepare for the next day's mission to Palm Beach.

With Valerie balanced on her hip, Betty helped Jim pack into his bag the last few items for the mission. Among them were things that might amuse an Auca visitor. Since Jim knew only enough of their language to have a two-minute conversation, he felt he needed some other way to hold their attention and show them he was friendly. He packed a harmonica, a View-Master with several different picture reels, and a yo-yo. He also tucked a gun into the side pocket of his bag. The men had spent a long time discussing whether or not they should take guns. After all, they were going in the name of God, the King of Peace. What would the Aucas think of the gospel if the missionaries brought guns? In the end, they all decided common sense required them to arm themselves. There would be many dangerous animals—pumas, alligators, and snakes—around Palm Beach, and the men wanted a means of protection. In addition, they agreed that if the Aucas did attack them, they could fire over the attackers' heads as a last resort. The members of the team promised each other that on no account would they shoot directly at the Aucas. If it came to a choice between losing their own lives and taking the life of an Auca, the missionaries were ready to lay down their lives.

Before Jim and Betty had had time to say a proper good-bye, the yellow Piper Cruiser was buzzing overhead. It was time for Jim to leave. Jim and Betty walked to the airstrip, and when Nate Saint brought the plane to a halt, Jim loaded his things into the back of it. Jim kissed Betty, hugged Valerie, and climbed into the cockpit beside Nate. Minutes later, he was peering down at Shandia. As he and Nate headed for Arajuno, Jim caught a glimpse of his wife and little girl.

By nightfall, Jim Elliot, Nate Saint, Ed McCully, Roger Youderian, and Pete Fleming, who had finally decided to go on the mission, were all gathered at Arajuno. As they made their final plans, the mood was a strange mix of exhilaration and somberness. The men were excited about what lay ahead but also mindful of the potential danger. They made lists of everything that would need to be transported to Palm Beach and then marked each item with a number code according to its priority. Those items marked with a 1 would be needed first, consisting mostly of the materials required for building the tree house. Everyone had agreed on the importance of a safe shelter by nightfall. The handcranked radio also had a 1 beside it. Communication with the outside world was vital right from the start.

The number 2 next to an item meant the item would be important to have as the day wore on, such as a pot to cook dinner in, coffee mugs, and air mattresses. The number 3 was for things like notepaper, books, and magazines, which would come in handy once the mission was established on Palm Beach.

Jim, Ed, Nate, Roger, and Pete talked long into the night until there was nothing left to say. In the early morning hours, Jim lay in bed trying to imagine what would happen by the end of that day. Would the Aucas visit them? Would he have the opportunity to look an Auca warrior in the eye, smile, and be able to show him he'd come in peace? If he did, the missionaries would be the first group in history to meet Aucas face-to-face and live to tell about it. And if not... Jim chose not to dwell on that possibility. Yet whatever happened, he knew they had taken every precaution possible. Now, as always, his life and the lives of his four missionary companions were in God's hands.

Jim was awakened the next morning by the squeal of a boiling kettle. For a moment, he couldn't remember what he was doing at the McCully house, and then it came back to him with a flood of excitement. Today was the day! He quickly got up, got dressed, and bounded into the living room. He glanced at his watch. It was six-thirty, only an hour and a half before Nate was scheduled to take off for Palm Beach. Since they had packed everything the night before, the five men sat down to a hearty breakfast, but Jim was too excited to eat much.

After breakfast, it was time to help Nate weigh

cargo and load the plane. Every ounce of cargo had to be accounted for. Each extra pound of weight meant the Piper needed an extra foot of runway on which to land and take off. It was going to be tight at Palm Beach, even without extra weight to worry about. It would be a disaster to overload the plane and end up running into the Curaray River.

Nate wanted to be extra cautious, insisting on taking only one passenger on each trip. The men drew straws to determine who the first passenger would be. Ed McCully won, but winning the draw was a dubious honor. So many things could go wrong on the first landing. If, for instance, the sand was too soft or the plane was damaged in the landing, Ed and Nate would be stranded in the heart of Auca territory. They would have no other option but to walk out to Arajuno, and that would prove difficult because they knew of no paths to follow. Being in their neighbors' backyard would also be dangerous, since the Aucas did not have a record of being kind to people who strayed into their territory! The five men gathered on the airstrip for a brief prayer. Then Jim stood back with Roger Youderian and Pete Fleming while Nate Saint, with Ed McCully tucked in the seat beside him, cranked the Piper Cruiser's engine to life. Operation Auca had entered its final stage!

An hour later, Nate returned to Arajuno. As he climbed from the cockpit, he announced that things had gone okay, though not quite according to plan. A heavy fog had developed about two miles out from Palm Beach, but Nate had been able to find a spot where it thinned enough for him to locate the landing site. The sand on Palm Beach had been softer than Nate had expected, causing the plane's tires to dig into the sand. Nate and Ed had manually turned the plane around and pushed its tail out over the water so that Nate would have enough distance to take off. Despite these unexpected events, Ed was safely on the beach and waiting anxiously for Nate to return with the second load.

Nate let some air out of the tires to keep them from digging into the sand of Palm Beach as much as on the first trip. Jim hoped it would work; he was on the next flight.

By the time Nate and Jim were airborne on the second trip to Palm Beach, the sun had driven off the fog. It was a beautiful, clear morning over the Oriente. Within minutes, the plane was following the Curaray River as it snaked through the dense jungle. Finally, with the sun glinting on the river, Jim caught his first glimpse of Palm Beach. The strip of sand was wider than he had imagined, but shorter! Jim marveled that Nate had been able to land and take off from it. Nate was quite a pilot.

From above, Jim and Nate scoured the riverbank for Ed McCully.

"There he is," said Jim with relief, pointing toward the far end of the beach.

Jim gripped the edge of his seat until his knuckles were white as Nate calmly and expertly guided the Piper Cruiser down onto the beach. The partially flattened tires did a great job. The wheels thumped against the sand but did not dig in. Nate brought the plane to a halt a few feet from the trees at the end of the beach. Ed bounded over to the plane, the home-movie camera in his hand still rolling. With a huge grin, Jim jumped from the cockpit.

The plane stayed only long enough to drop off Jim and the load of supplies. After Jim and Ed had picked up the Piper's tail and turned it around, Nate gunned the engine and took off for Arajuno to collect Roger and another load of cargo. He had a tight schedule to keep if they were going to get everything they had planned done before dark.

When Nate returned, Roger jumped out and, along with Jim and Ed, helped unload the cargo, which included several days' supply of food. As soon as the plane was empty, Nate was on his way again.

The men went straight to work. Jim and Ed had already selected the tree they thought was most suitable for their tree house. It was a giant iron-wood tree about two hundred feet tall. About thirty-five feet up, a wide branch fanned out, providing what looked like a solid foundation on which to perch their temporary new home.

Jim began the task of nailing strips of wood up the tree to use as steps. Each man took turns standing guard while the other two hammered away. As the steps got higher up the tree, one of the men threw a rope over a lower branch to use as a harness. The last thing they needed was for one of them to slip and fall. It took a surprising amount of time for them to nail all the steps into the tree. It was clear why these trees had been named ironwood. The work was remarkably like trying to drive spikes into iron. Still, the crew persevered, and once they reached the branch, Jim was satisfied it would do nicely for the tree house. Jim tied a rope to the branch and lowered it to the ground, where Ed attached precut lengths of timber. Jim and Roger pulled the planks one at a time up into the tree and nailed them in place.

As the tree house progressed, Nate made two more flights to deliver materials and supplies. On the last flight, he brought Pete Fleming with him. Pete and Nate unloaded the plane and then began stacking and arranging all the supplies.

Since the tree house had been designed and precut to sleep three people, someone was going to have to fly out each night to Arajuno with Nate. Since Pete was the lightest man in the group, Nate decided he would be the one to accompany him each night. The lighter the load, the better for taking off from tiny Palm Beach.

As the sun began to sink low on the horizon, the five men gathered on the beach to sing a hymn together. They then said a short prayer, and Nate and Pete climbed into the plane and took off. Jim watched in amazement as Nate skillfully guided the Piper into the air from such a narrow strip of sand.

Jim, Ed, and Roger stood on the beach talking.

Ten minutes later, they heard the buzz of the airplane's engine. The men had planned for Nate to circle Terminal City and for Pete to deliver the message "Come to the Curaray tomorrow" in Auca over the loudspeaker. Nate dipped the plane's wings as a signal that the message had been delivered. Then he looped around and headed west toward Arajuno.

Jim, Ed, and Roger prepared dinner, which they ate as they sat around a small campfire. Before it got dark, they climbed up into the tree house. As the three men settled down for the night, they wondered who might be watching from the cover of the jungle.

At two o'clock in the morning, Jim still lay awake. The suffocatingly hot night kept him from sleeping, as did the fact that he couldn't stretch his tall frame out properly without banging against the low wall of the tree house. He wished he'd added another six inches to the length of the planks when he cut them.

Jim listened to the breathing of his two companions, who sounded as if they were not asleep either. They weren't. The three of them decided it was time for a coffee break. The evening before, the men had packed a few sandwiches and filled a thermos with coffee, just in case they couldn't sleep. They ate and drank in relative silence, straining their ears to listen for unfamiliar sounds.

After what seemed like an eternal night, dawn broke over the jungle, and the men climbed down for breakfast. Jim noted puma tracks in the sand that had not been there the night before. At 9:00 he cranked up the radio, but to his dismay he couldn't send out a transmission on it. He could hear people on it, but they couldn't seem to hear him. So he just listened to the daily round of morning conversation between the various mission stations and Shell Mera. One station needed an extra bag of flour, another more antibiotics, while a third inquired as to whether a specific package had shown up in the mail. The voices on the radio made everything seem strangely normal, except for one thing: Jim, Ed, and Roger were right in the middle of Auca territory.

When the transmissions were over, the men continued with Operation Auca. Each man took a position along the beach and then took turns holding up gifts and yelling Auca phrases. At every crackle of a branch or rustle of a bush, they paused. Could it be an Auca, or was it a puma? As the morning wore on, they saw neither.

Before lunch, Nate and Pete flew in with encouraging news. When they had flown over Terminal City that morning on their way to Palm Beach, they had seen hardly a person. Perhaps a ground party was on its way to meet the missionaries. Jim was exuberant. Today could be the day!

The five men tried to busy themselves with other tasks while they waited. Nate quickly discovered why the radio would not transmit—the microphone had a loose connection. The men built a makeshift roof over the fire and cooking area to give them shelter from the relentless sun as it hung overhead at midday. They also took turns napping, swimming, reading, and keeping watch for their neighbors. But no one saw anything. Finally, late in the afternoon, Jim, Ed, and Roger wrote notes to their wives. Nate and Pete collected the mail with a promise to deliver it when they flew to Arajuno in the evening.

That night, before climbing up to the tree house, Jim placed a machete at the bottom of the steps. He hoped that if the Aucas came in the night, they would find it and understand it was another gift.

The three men woke sharply at 9:00 p.m. Jim could feel his heart thumping in his chest. He looked around. "Did you hear something?" he whispered.

In the moonlight, he could see his two companions nod. Then he heard the noise again—a long, low creak.

After a few minutes, Jim relaxed. The wind had picked up since they had gone to bed, and the noise they were hearing was the planks of their tree house shifting in the swaying tree. The three men drifted back to sleep.

Jim awoke again at 5:00 a.m., just before daybreak. He was anxious to see whether someone had collected the machete from the bottom of the tree. He shined his flashlight down the thirty-five feet to the jungle floor. The machete was gone! Jim's whoop of joy woke Ed and Roger, who celebrated with Jim. Then Ed took the flashlight and shined it down to see for himself. This time the tip of the machete glistened in the beam of light. A huge leaf had blown down and covered most of the machete. Disappointment clouded Jim's face.

While they waited for Nate and Pete to arrive, the men ate breakfast and held a prayer meeting. Then Jim decided it was time to catch some fish for lunch. He stripped to the waist, found his fishing pole, and waded into the river. Every so often he would continue his one-sided conversation with the Aucas. Just as he was reeling in a good-sized catfish, he heard the familiar buzz of the Piper Cruiser's engine. Shortly, Nate and Pete were on the ground telling them more hopeful news.

Nate had seen footprints on a small beach upriver! The Aucas must be nearby after all. The group ate lunch with one eye on the jungle. No one knew how old the tracks were, but if they were recent, the Aucas could burst into view at any moment. Still, no visitors appeared during lunch, and Jim was beginning to find the waiting much harder than he'd anticipated. He felt like a coiled spring just waiting to be let go.

After lunch, Jim and Pete set off upriver to investigate the footprints more thoroughly. They stopped frequently to study the many tracks from tapirs, birds, alligators, and pumas that crisscrossed the sand, a clear reminder that the jungle belonged more to the animals than to anyone else.

"Hey Jim, over here," called Pete.

Jim came running. Sure enough, Pete had found human footprints. The prints seemed to have been made by an adult, a child, and a toddler. To Jim and Pete's dismay, the footprints had deep cracks running through them. Neither Jim nor Pete knew as much as the Quichua Indians knew about reading footprints, but they had learned that deep cracks meant that the prints were old, perhaps as much as a week. It seemed unlikely that the footprints belonged to potential visitors to their campsite. Besides, it was highly doubtful that anyone coming to meet the missionaries would bring a toddler.

Dispirited, Jim and Pete waded back downstream to tell the others the disappointing news.

When Jim and Pete arrived back at camp, they found Nate, Ed, and Roger swimming. Underwater the men were at least able to get some relief from the thousands of flying insects that swarmed around the camp.

The rest of Thursday passed much the same as Wednesday. For the third night, Nate and Pete flew back to Arajuno, and after dinner, Jim, Ed, and Roger climbed up to their tree house without any sign of the Aucas.

As Jim drifted off to sleep, he prayed that the following day would bring an opportunity to finally meet the mysterious tribe face-to-face.

Chapter 15

Visitors at Last

Friday, January 6: The day started ordinarily enough. Nate and Pete flew in around midmorning. By the time they arrived, the three other men had taken up their usual positions. Ed was upstream a little from Palm Beach, Roger was in the middle, and Jim was a little downstream. Each man took turns yelling Auca phrases into the vast greenery.

Jim was in the midst of yelling *"Bito weka pomopa"* when a male voice rang across the water and said in Auca, "We have come."

Someone had answered from the jungle!

Jim watched transfixed as the leaves rustled and three naked figures emerged from the tangled jungle. The first to step into the open was a man. Jim guessed he was about twenty years old. The man was quickly followed by a slightly older woman and then a teenage girl. The two groups stared at each other across the Curaray River. For a moment, there was total silence, and then the realization of what was happening sank in. In unison, Jim, Ed, and Roger yelled across the river to their guests, "*Poinani!*" (you're here), the Auca way of welcoming one another.

The Auca man, probably thinking the missionaries spoke fluent Auca, began a long speech. As he spoke, he kept pushing the teenage girl toward the men. It was obvious to Jim that the man was trying to offer her as some kind of gift or exchange.

Finally, the man stopped talking, and it seemed to Jim the next move belonged to the missionaries. If they didn't do something, the three Aucas might slip back into the jungle.

"I'm going over to get them," Jim yelled to Ed as he quickly unbuttoned his shirt, pulled off his shoes, and waded eagerly into the water.

"Slow down, slow down. You might frighten them," Nate yelled after him.

Jim eased up his pace. As he reached the far shore, the teenage girl jumped off the log she was standing on and splashed her way over to meet him. Jim held out his hand, which she grasped. Then Jim reached for the other two Aucas. The man grasped Jim's hand, and Jim led the group across the river to the camp.

Jim watched carefully for any signs that the Aucas might be frightened or violent, but he saw none. Instead, the visitors squatted comfortably around the campfire and began to chatter to each other.

Jim recognized a few words but not many. However, with the help of the phrases he had collected on index cards, Jim was confident he could make the Aucas understand they were welcome.

Roger reached into the box of kitchen equipment and found a paring knife. He handed it to the Auca man, who grinned with pleasure. After examining it closely, the man carefully placed the knife on the ground between his feet. Next, Nate unveiled a model he'd made of his Piper Cruiser. All five men watched eagerly for the Aucas' reaction. Would the visitors understand the connection between their hosts, the airplane, and the gifts that had descended on Terminal City?

Again, the Auca man simply grinned and nodded. He seemed to understand just fine. So all eight people—the missionaries and the Aucas—sat together on the beach for about an hour, trying to communicate with each other. As that continued, the missionaries talked among themselves about their Auca guests and assigned them nicknames. The Auca man was called George, and the teenage girl, Delilah.

Since the guests did not seem to be afraid, Jim and Nate pulled out cameras and took many photos. Some of the funniest photos were those that captured the expressions on the two women's faces as they flipped through a copy of *Time* magazine Ed had brought. Jim couldn't begin to imagine what crossed those Stone Age minds when confronted with pictures of refrigerators laden with food and the latest Ford automobile.

After a while, Delilah stood up and walked slowly over to the airplane. She rubbed her body against the course yellow canvas on its fuselage. Soon, the other two Aucas joined her, and George began to gesture excitedly. As astonished as the five missionaries were, George's message was clear. He wanted a ride in the plane. After a quick conference, Nate agreed to take him up and fly over Terminal City. Nate had a few concerns, though. What if George got bored during the flight and decided to climb out? Or what if he grabbed the plane's yoke and would not let go? Still, the risks were worth taking, especially since George seemed to be indicating he would use the plane ride to invite other Auca tribesmen to visit the campsite.

Nate found a shirt for George to wear, since it would be much cooler in the air than on the ground, and buttoned him into it. George grinned with satisfaction. After placing the paring knife and a machete the missionaries had given him into the plane, George climbed happily into the front seat. Nate hitched up the safety belt, and they were ready for takeoff. George was about to become the first Auca to fly!

Jim watched as the Piper climbed off the sandy beach and disappeared over the treetops. He then turned his attention back to Delilah and the older

Auca woman. The four men watched in amusement as the two women tried their hand at blowing up balloons and playing with a yo-yo.

About fifteen minutes later, the Piper Cruiser flew back into view. Jim could see George clearly, who was leaning out the doorway, waving and shouting. Things had apparently gone well.

The plane made a perfect landing on the sand. After Nate had undone the seat belt, George jumped out and ran over to the group where he chattered away in Auca. He was no doubt telling the two women what it was like to be in an airplane.

As George talked to the women, Nate filled the other missionaries in on the flight. All had gone well, and although George never stopped yelling and waving throughout the flight, he had been a perfect passenger. The man had even stayed buckled in his seat—Nate surmised that George didn't know how to work the buckle—and he had not touched the controls once. But best of all, as Nate had swooped in low over Terminal City, George had yelled down to the Aucas below. Nate wasn't 100 percent sure what he said, but he recognized enough words to know that George was inviting the others to visit the campsite on the Curaray River.

"You should have seen their faces!" Nate chuckled as he went on recounting the events of the flight. "They couldn't believe it when they saw George in the plane! One woman in shock dropped the basket she was carrying."

The five men all laughed. Things were going better than expected. The missionaries had made contact with three friendly Aucas, and now one of them had been able to tell other Aucas it was safe to visit.

Pete and Ed prepared hamburgers for lunch while the Aucas looked on. When the hamburgers were cooked, the missionaries offered one to each of their guests. The three Aucas took the hamburgers gratefully and devoured them in just a few bites. They then put out their hands for more. After two more hamburgers each, the guests focused on the next thing: strawberry cake with lemon frosting that Marilou McCully had sent in with Nate and Pete that morning.

The rest of the day passed quickly. Before long, it was time for Nate and Pete to head back to Arajuno. As they were preparing to leave, Jim collected all the film they had shot that day and placed it into a canvas bag. Nate loaded the bag into the Piper. Although a sobering thought, if anything were to happen to the men on Palm Beach, at least the photographic record of their historic meeting with the Aucas would be safe.

After sharing a pot of baked beans and some rolls for dinner, Jim motioned to their guests that the three missionaries would soon be climbing up to the tree house to sleep. He then invited the Aucas to spend the night on the beach around the fire and under the roof of their cooking area. The Aucas seemed to understand, but Delilah was obviously upset about the arrangement. She stood up, collected her gifts, and stomped off down the beach. George yelled after her, but she did not turn back. He shrugged his shoulders as if to say, "Women—who can understand them?" before collecting his things and trotting off after her.

The older Auca woman did not follow. She appeared to think it was her duty to stay and explain the situation. She spent ten minutes talking to Roger at top speed. Roger did not catch a single word of what she said, but the woman seemed to calm down once she had gotten it off her chest. The woman indicated that she would stay and sleep by the fire, and that is where the men left her.

As best as a person in a cramped tree house thirty-five feet off the ground can, Jim bounded out of bed the next morning. His mind was crystal clear. Today, for certain, was the day they were going to meet more Aucas. Jim quickly dressed and climbed down from the tree house, anxious to see whether the older woman was still there and whether George and Delilah had returned.

When Jim got to the beach, he was disappointed. The older woman was nowhere to be seen, nor was George or Delilah. Jim picked up a stick and raked the embers of the fire, which still glowed red. He found some encouragement in that. The older woman must have stayed most of the night and stoked the fire, and felt safe doing so.

It was Saturday, January 7. At around 9:00 a.m., Nate and Pete arrived from Arajuno. Together, the five men waited excitedly for more Aucas to arrive. Morning gave way to afternoon, but no one arrived. Their hopes began to fade with the late afternoon sun. Dejected, Nate and Pete climbed back into the plane and headed out for the night. As Jim, Ed, and Roger prepared dinner, they discussed possible reasons why the Aucas had not come. If George and Delilah had returned to the rest of the Aucas, why hadn't they convinced them to come and visit? Surely the others would want their own machete and even a plane ride? No matter how the men tried to explain it, it just didn't seem to make any sense why more Aucas hadn't come.

The Piper Cruiser touched down around lunchtime Sunday, the sixth day of homesteading at Palm Beach. Nate jumped from the cockpit with a large picnic hamper, the sight of which greatly cheered Jim, Ed, and Roger. Marilou McCully had sent more treats for them.

As they all devoured the muffins and ice cream, Nate and Pete delivered some great news. On the way in from Arajuno, they had flown over Terminal City, where they had seen only a handful of women and children. Then, about halfway to Palm Beach, Nate and Pete had spotted more Aucas. A group of about ten men was walking determinedly toward the treehouse. The missionaries were about to have more Auca visitors at Palm Beach. The men whooped and hollered with delight as they finished their muffins and ice cream. Sunday, January 8, 1956, was going to be a day to remember!

At 12:30 p.m. Nate cranked up the radio and relayed the good news to Marj at Shell Mera, using code words, of course. He promised to call back at 4:30 and give an update. If his calculations were correct, their new visitors would have been with them for about two hours by then.

After three o'clock, Jim spotted the first of their new guests. Three Auca women had emerged from the undergrowth on the far side of the river. Jim motioned to Pete, and together they began to wade across to meet them. Jim and Pete repeated friendly Auca phrases, but the women did not appear to be as neighborly as the previous Auca visitors. The faces of the women remained blank, and the women did not try to talk back to the missionaries.

Jim and Pete were nearly to the far side of the Curaray River when they heard a bloodcurdling cry behind them. They turned to see a swarm of Auca warriors, their long spears ready to strike, running across the beach toward Nate, Ed, and Roger. Jim stood transfixed for a moment, his hand on the gun in his pocket. Should he use it? Even before he'd processed the question, he knew the answer. Each of them had promised the other they would not kill to save themselves from being killed. They would not kill those they came to share the gospel with in the name of Jesus.

Within seconds, Nate Saint had been speared. As he fell to the ground, his arm smashed against a rock, breaking his watch. The hands of the watch stopped at 3:10 p.m. As Ed McCully rushed over to help, a spear was thrust into his back. Ed slumped onto the sandy beach beside Nate.

Jim scanned the scene for Roger Youderian. Out of the corner of his eye, he saw Roger running toward the airplane, probably trying to get to the radio to call Marj for help. In reality, there was no help for them. No one would be able to arrive in time. Having killed Nate and Ed, the Auca warriors sprinted into the water. Pete Fleming scrambled up onto a log and yelled as best he could in Auca, "We came to meet you. We aren't going to hurt you. Why are you killing us?"

Those were the last words Jim Elliot heard on this earth. Within seconds, a spear had been thrust into Jim, who splashed facedown into the water. The gentle current of the Curaray River flowing past Palm Beach nudged his body downstream.

Chapter 16

One Great Purpose

At 4:30 in the afternoon, Betty Elliot waited by the radio at Shandia to hear the transmission between Marj and Nate Saint. She, like all the wives of the men in Operation Auca, were eager to hear whether the Aucas had arrived and, if so, what they were doing. Were they as friendly as George and the two women? Had Nate taken any more of them up flying? Was Jim learning more Auca words?

The hands on the wall clock crawled past 4:30, then 4:40, then 4:45. With increasing apprehension, Betty fidgeted by the radio. She got Valerie up from her afternoon nap and mashed some vegetables for her daughter's dinner. Still, no message on the radio. Finally, Betty radioed Marj Saint just in case she had somehow missed the message from Palm

Beach. Marj had heard nothing, but she would let Betty know as soon as she did hear.

Finally darkness fell across the jungle of the Oriente. Before Betty climbed into bed, she radioed Marj one last time. Still no news, and Nate and Pete had not arrived at Arajuno for the night. At first light, Johnny Keenan would fly over Palm Beach to see what the problem might be.

Johnny Keenan was apprehensive as he guided his Piper Pacer off the airstrip at Shell Mera and banked in an easterly direction toward Palm Beach. As he picked up the Curaray River and followed its meandering course through the jungle, he tried to think positively, but it was hard not to imagine the worst. As Johnny flew over Palm Beach, he became aware that the worst had indeed happened.

From the air, Johnny could see the yellow Piper Cruiser at the end of the beach. The plane had been stripped bare, as though it were a carcass that had been descended upon by vultures. Strips of shredded yellow canvas lay like streamers on the wet sand.

Johnny looped around and flew over the beach again, but he could see no sign of the men. Again, he tried to think positively. Perhaps they had fled into the jungle and were making their way to Arajuno. But as he looked down at the broken remains of Nate's plane, he had a sick feeling inside that something worse had happened to the five men. He turned the nose of his plane in the direction of Shell Mera. He had some difficult news to share with the anxious wives.

Back at Shell Mera, no one was ready to give up hope. Since Johnny Keenan hadn't seen any sign of the men, it was possible they were still alive, either hiding in the jungle or being held against their will by the Aucas. Yet, in the back of everyone's mind was the disturbing fact that the Aucas didn't seem to take prisoners, choosing instead to kill.

By late Monday night, the secret Operation Auca was headline news around the world. Newspapers were emblazoned with headlines like "Missionaries Missing Among Jungle Savages," "Five Missionaries Massacred?" "American Men Meet a Violent End Among a Stone Age Tribe?"

People began to converge on Shell Mera in an attempt to locate some sign of the missionaries. A United States military rescue team headed by Air Force Major Malcolm Nurnberg and consisting of three planes and a helicopter was ordered to Shell Mera from its base in Panama to help with the search. The president of the Missionary Aviation Fellowship arrived from California. Soon afterward, two officials from Christian Missions in Many Lands, the Plymouth Brethren mission agency with which Jim Elliot, Pete Fleming, and Ed McCully served, also arrived. Sam Saint, Nate Saint's brother, was an experienced pilot with American Airlines and came to help with the rescue effort. Two of the world's top magazines, *Life* and *Time,* dispatched their veteran reporters and photographers to cover the unfolding story.

Abe Van Der Puy, from the missionary radio station HJCB in Quito, came down to help and support Marj Saint, who by now was running a full-scale airport control tower from Shell Mera. He took on the job of coordinating the press releases for which the world seemed to be clamoring.

Johnny Keenan flew out and picked up Betty and Valerie Elliot from Shandia and brought them to Shell Mera. He did the same for the other wives, until all five women and their children were gathered together.

Wednesday morning, three days after the attack, the first two bodies were spotted from an Air Force helicopter. Since they were floating facedown in the water, it was impossible to be sure who they were.

While the air search continued for the remaining bodies, a search party made its way by canoe down the Curaray River to Palm Beach. The party consisted of several missionaries who knew Nate Saint well and thirteen Ecuadorian soldiers who had been assigned to help with the recovery efforts. The search party was led by Frank Drown, a veteran missionary in the Oriente and Roger Youderian's former coworker among the Jivaro Indians at Macuma.

On Thursday, January 12, 1956, four long days after the last radio contact with the men, Major Nurnberg walked slowly into Shell Mera. He asked Marj Saint if there was somewhere private the five wives could meet, preferably without the children. Marj led Barbara Youderian, Marilou McCully, Olive Fleming, and Betty Elliot into her bedroom.

Major Nurnberg cleared his throat and squared his shoulders as he entered the room. He officially confirmed the awful truth: The five men were dead. Four bodies had been spotted from the air. The major flipped open his notebook and checked his notes. He described articles of clothing rescuers had seen on the bodies. One body was wearing a woven red belt.

"That's Pete," said Olive Fleming, quietly.

Another had on a tee-shirt and pair of blue jeans. Barbara Youderian identified Roger's jungle "uniform."

One body, caught under an overhanging tree, had only a gray sock visible. The rest of the wives could not identify whether that was Jim Elliot, Ed McCully, or Nate Saint. They would have to wait until the search party arrived by canoe and properly identified the remaining bodies.

The next day, Friday, Frank Drown's search party finally arrived at Palm Beach. Soon after, the Air Force helicopter was hovering overhead. As the Ecuadorian soldiers guarded the perimeter of Palm Beach, the helicopter guided the other members of the search party to the bodies. The Aucas had apparently dragged the bodies into the Curaray River. The dead missionaries had been swept downstream and were now floating facedown in the muddy water. The first body recovered was that of Roger Youderian, then Jim Elliot, Nate Saint, and finally Pete Fleming. The search party looked everywhere but could not locate Ed McCully's body, which was never found and presumably had been washed farther downstream. There was ample evidence, though, that Ed had been killed with the others.

Fearing for their own safety, the men in the search party hurriedly dug a communal grave on the beach. Frank Drown pulled off the men's watches and wedding rings and removed the contents of their pockets before respectfully lowering the bodies into the grave. He would take those personal belongings back to the grieving widows.

A large tropical storm was gathering, and the first crash of thunder boomed just as the brief funeral service got under way. The service took only a few minutes, but by the time it was over, the rain was pouring down. Once the grave was covered, it was time for everyone to leave. With their guns cocked and eyes alert for any movement in the undergrowth, the members of the search party pushed their canoes into the Curaray River and headed back upstream to safety.

On Saturday, the day after the funeral service, a Navy R-4D aircraft from the U.S. military rescue team flew the five wives over Palm Beach so that the women could see for the first time where their husbands had labored, had died, and were now buried. The sun shone brightly on the white, sandy beach. Strips of yellow canvas still littered the area. Betty could see the cooking shelter Jim and the others had built. The ashes of the fire the men had sat around while waiting for the Aucas to arrive—the moment those men had planned and prayed for so diligently—were still visible.

News of the death of the five young missionaries in the jungle of eastern Ecuador reverberated around the world. When people heard of the death of Jim Elliot, a strong, intelligent twenty-eight-year-old, they questioned why God would allow him and his four equally talented and dedicated companions to be killed. Surely God could have prevented it. Why didn't He? Even today, no one can fully answer that question. It is probable, though, that in death, Jim Elliot, Pete Fleming, Ed McCully, Roger Youderian, and Nate Saint did more to challenge Christians around the world as to the need for missionaries than could have been accomplished in two lifetimes. Jim Elliot's life was and is a vivid reminder to Christians of all walks of life to live every day with one great purpose in mind: share the gospel message with those who have not yet heard it.

Epilogue

The story of the Aucas didn't stop with the deaths of the five men at Palm Beach. Johnny Keenan and Hobey Lowrance, the MAF pilot who came to Shell Mera to replace Nate Saint, continued dropping gifts over the Auca settlement. Rachel Saint continued her work with Dayuma to learn the Auca language. Betty Elliot and eleven-month-old Valerie returned to Shandia and the important work among the Quichua Indians. All of them, and many more Christians around the world, prayed that one day the opportunity to share the gospel message with the Aucas would come.

In November 1957, twenty-two months after the killings at Palm Beach, two Auca women walked out of the jungle and into a Quichua fishing village, a six-hour trek from Arajuno, where Betty Elliot was visiting. As soon as Betty heard this, she set out to meet them. Betty persuaded the two women to return to Shandia with her. Their names were Mintaka and Mankamu. Mintaka was the older Auca woman who had accompanied George and Delilah to visit the men at Palm Beach. Betty soon learned that the women had come searching for Dayuma, whose mother was getting old and wanted to see her again.

At the time the women were looking for her, Dayuma was traveling with Rachel Saint to the United States. During the trip, Dayuma became a Christian. When Rachel and Dayuma finally returned from their journey, they met with Mintaka and Mankamu. On September 3, 1958, Dayuma and the two Auca women set out to rejoin their tribe.

Three weeks later, Dayuma, Mintaka, Mankamu, and seven other Aucas again appeared at Arajuno. They came to invite Rachel Saint, Betty Elliot, and Valerie Elliot to come and live among them in their jungle village. The Aucas wanted to hear more about the God Dayuma had described to them. The opportunity to share the gospel face-to-face with the Aucas, for whom the men of Operation Auca had given their lives, had finally arrived. On October 6, 1958, Betty and Valerie Elliot, Rachel Saint, and their Auca entourage headed into the Amazon jungle.

Betty and Valerie Elliot remained among the Waorani for two years. (*Waorani* was the name the Aucas called themselves in their own language. *Auca* was a derogatory name given to them by the Quichua Indians.)

Rachel Saint spent the rest of her life among the Waorani. She died among them in 1994 and was buried not far from Palm Beach, thirty-eight years after the men of Operation Auca had been laid to rest there.

After her eventual return to the United States, Betty Elliot chronicled the story of Operation Auca and the events at Palm Beach in the best-selling book, *Through Gates of Splendor*. Decades later, the story of the death of five young missionaries at Palm Beach, in the jungle of the Oriente, continues to impact Christian readers the world over with a ringing challenge: take the gospel to those who live in darkness without the saving knowledge of Jesus Christ.

Bibliography

Elliot, Elisabeth, *Shadow of the Almighty,* HarperCollins Publishers, 1957.

Elliot, Elisabeth, *Through Gates of Splendor,* Tyndale House Publishers, 1981.

Hitt, Russell T., *Jungle Pilot,* Discovery House Publishers, 1959.

Miller, Susan Martins, *Jim Elliot: Missionary to Ecuador,* Barbour Publishing, Inc., 1995.

White, Kathleen, *Jim Elliot,* Bethany House Publishers, 1990.

About the Authors

Janet and Geoff Benge are a husband and wife writing team with more than thirty years of writing experience. Janet is a former elementary school teacher. Geoff holds a degree in history. Originally from New Zealand, the Benges spent ten years serving with Youth With A Mission. They have two daughters, Laura and Shannon, and an adopted son, Lito. They make their home in the Orlando, Florida, area.

Also from Janet and Geoff Benge…

More adventure-filled biographies for ages 10 to 100!

Heroes of History

George Washington Carver: From Slave to Scientist • 978-1-883002-78-7
Abraham Lincoln: A New Birth of Freedom • 978-1-883002-79-4
Meriwether Lewis: Off the Edge of the Map • 978-1-883002-80-0
George Washington: True Patriot • 978-1-883002-81-7
William Penn: Liberty and Justice for All • 978-1-883002-82-4
Harriet Tubman: Freedombound • 978-1-883002-90-9
John Adams: Independence Forever • 978-1-883002-50-3
Clara Barton: Courage under Fire • 978-1-883002-51-0
Daniel Boone: Frontiersman • 978-1-932096-09-5
Theodore Roosevelt: An American Original • 978-1-932096-10-1
Douglas MacArthur: What Greater Honor • 978-1-932096-15-6
Benjamin Franklin: Live Wire • 978-1-932096-14-9
Christopher Columbus: Across the Ocean Sea • 978-1-932096-23-1
Laura Ingalls Wilder: A Storybook Life • 978-1-932096-32-3
Orville Wright: The Flyer • 978-1-932096-34-7
Captain John Smith: A Foothold in the New World • 978-1-932096-36-1
Thomas Edison: Inspiration and Hard Work • 978-1-932096-37-8
Alan Shepard: Higher and Faster • 978-1-932096-41-5
Ronald Reagan: Destiny at His Side • 978-1-932096-65-1
Davy Crockett: Ever Westward • 978-1-932096-67-5
Milton Hershey: More Than Chocolate • 978-1-932096-82-8
Billy Graham: America's Pastor • 978-1-62486-024-9
Ben Carson: A Chance at Life • 978-1-62486-034-8
Louis Zamperini: Redemption • 978-1-62486-049-2
Elizabeth Fry: Angel of Newgate • 978-1-62486-064-5
William Wilberforce: Take Up the Fight • 978-1-62486-057-7
William Bradford: Plymouth's Rock • 978-1-62486-092-8
Ernest Shackleton: Going South • 978-1-62486-093-5
Benjamin Rush: The Common Good • 978-1-62486-123-9

Available in paperback, e-book, and audiobook formats.
Unit Study Curriculum Guides are available for many biographies.
www.Emeraldbooks.com

Christian Heroes: Then & Now
GLADYS AYLWARD
The Adventure of a Lifetime
JANET & GEOFF BENGE

Christian Heroes: Then & Now
GLADYS AYLWARD
The Adventure of a Lifetime
JANET & GEOFF BENGE
YWAM

Christian Heroes: Then & Now
Audio Heroes
GLADYS AYLWARD
The Adventure of a Lifetime
JANET & GEOFF BENGE

Christian Heroes: Then & Now
GEORGE MÜLLER
The Guardian of Bristol's Orphans
JANET & GEOFF BENGE

Christian Heroes: Then & Now
GEORGE MÜLLER
The Guardian of Bristol's Orphans
JANET & GEOFF BENGE
YWAM

Christian Heroes: Then & Now
Audio Heroes
GEORGE MÜLLER
The Guardian of Bristol's Orphans
JANET & GEOFF BENGE